# "Value-Driven Leadership"

*The power of Servant Leadership with Teach, Model, & Coach*

By

Troy C. Smith

# Dedication

All glory to Jesus Christ, first and foremost, for modeling and inspiring me to become the man that God destined me to be. Furthermore, this is dedicated to my beautiful wife Jamie for all of her support, and love, through life's hills and valleys. Also to my mother Millicent Walcott, for having the strength and perseverance in raising a man the best she could!

I'm blessed! I thank you all!

# Acknowledgment

I would like to extend my deepest gratitude to my "Bad Boy" family that provided the "facts" to this TMC movement, and to all my friends/family for their unwavering support and encouragement throughout this journey. Your belief in me kept me going even when the path seemed unclear.

# Contents

# About the Author

Troy C. Smith is a dynamic inspirational speaker and servant leadership coach who embodies the principles of "Teach, Model, and Coach" in both his professional and personal life. A self-proclaimed "Student of Life," Troy's journey from a high school dropout in the Bronx, NY to GEICO's #1 Sales Manager nationwide is a testament to his resilience and determination. With over three decades of corporate experience, Troy's expertise in sales, leadership, and coaching is rooted in real-world challenges and triumphs.

His unique approach, blending humor with wisdom, captivates audiences and transforms mindsets. In 2023, Troy took a leap of faith, retiring from his decorated 24-year career at GEICO to pursue his calling as a full-time inspirational speaker and servant leadership coach. This decision, sparked by a vision involving recurring "2's," culminated in the launch of his company, TROY C. SMITH - Hope Inspirational Speaking LLC.

Beyond the podium, Troy is deeply committed to community service. He works closely with the United Way of Central Florida, volunteers as a Reading Pal, mentors as a "Big" with Big Brothers Big Sisters of Tampa Bay and co-leads a men's small group at Victory Church. These roles reflect his dedication to servant leadership and his mission of "Helping Other People Excel".

Troy's energetic messages of hope, grounded in clever acronyms, not only inspire but also provide practical strategies for personal and professional growth. His "Teach, Model, and Coach" methodology has proven effective in addressing modern workplace challenges, from employee retention to team collaboration.

With his John Maxwell Team certification and a wealth of life experiences, Troy C. Smith continues to electrify audiences, leaving them energized and ready for action. His story is not just one of personal success, but a roadmap for others to discover their potential and redefine success in an ever-evolving world.

# Chapter 1:
# In the Beginning

In the vast landscape of careers and aspirations, I found myself standing at the crossroads of ambition and uncertainty. The journey ahead promised challenges, but little did I know that it would be a transformative odyssey, one that would force me to confront the persistent leadership gaps that have plagued professionals for decades.

As I reflect on the beginning of my career, the memories are a blend of excitement and trepidation. As a high school dropout, I realized there would be endless challenges in a competitive world of sales in which facts validate one's success and existence. Armed with an array of life experience and a pocketful of dreams, I stepped into the corporate world, ready to conquer the challenges that lay ahead. Little did I realize that the landscape of leadership was riddled with gaps and crevices that demanded attention and introspection.

The first leadership gap that struck me was the lack of effective communication. In the rush to climb the corporate ladder, I often found myself struggling to convey my ideas clearly. Words seemed to jumble in my mind, and the gap between my intentions and the impact of my communication widened. I realized that effective leadership is not just about having a vision; it's about articulating that vision in a way that inspires and engages others.

The conference room was filled with the low hum of discussions as my colleagues gathered there annually for strategy meetings. Nervously, I scanned the room and took a deep breath. This was my chance to confront the first leadership obstacle: the lack of effective communication.

As the meeting kicked off, I consciously focused on my communication style. I began by acknowledging the importance of clear communication in achieving our shared goals. I shared a personal reflection, admitting that I had recognized a gap in my own communication and was committed to addressing it.

To bridge the divide between my intentions and the impact of my words, I introduced a new strategy. Instead of rushing through my ideas, I decided to slow down and organize my thoughts before speaking. I implemented a pause to gather my words, ensuring that my ideas were coherent and impactful.

Furthermore, I expressed my eagerness to receive feedback from my colleagues. I wanted to create an open dialogue where everyone felt comfortable sharing their thoughts on how to collectively enhance team communication. This gesture not only demonstrated humility but also emphasized the collaborative nature of effective leadership.

As the meeting progressed, I made a conscious effort to articulate my vision with clarity and enthusiasm. I used examples and anecdotes to illustrate key points, making the vision more relatable and inspiring to others. The change in my communication style did not go unnoticed, and the atmosphere in the room began to shift positively.

After the meeting, I encouraged one-on-one conversations with team members to gather more specific feedback and insights. This allowed me to address individual concerns and reinforced the idea that I was genuinely committed to improving communication within the team.

Another chasm that revealed itself early in my career was the absence of empathy. In a world driven by deadlines and targets, it was easy to lose sight of the human aspect of leadership. I observed leaders around me, and many seemed detached and focused solely on results. The gap between professional success and personal connection became apparent, prompting me to question the conventional wisdom that often separated the two.

As I navigated the complexities of my role, the third leadership gap emerged – a dearth of adaptability. The corporate landscape is dynamic and constantly evolving, and those who fail to adapt risk becoming obsolete. I found myself at times clinging to familiar strategies and routines, hesitant to embrace change. The gap between the known and the unknown, between comfort and growth, became a significant hurdle that demanded a shift in mindset.

The fourth gap that became glaringly evident was the lack of effective delegation. Early in my career, I often felt the weight of responsibilities on my shoulders, struggling to relinquish control. The gap between trust and control hindered not only my personal growth but also the growth of those around me. I began to realize that true leadership lies in empowering others and fostering an environment where everyone's strengths contribute to collective success.

Reflecting on these gaps, I couldn't help but see a pattern – a pattern that transcended my individual experiences and spoke to a broader systemic issue. These leadership gaps were not isolated incidents but pervasive challenges that echoed across industries and professions. The shortcomings in communication, empathy, adaptability, and delegation were like cracks in the foundation of leadership, threatening the stability of the structures built upon them.

The journey to bridge these gaps was not just a personal quest for improvement; it became a call to action. It prompted me to delve deeper into the roots of these leadership challenges, seeking not just solutions but a fundamental shift in perspective. It was time to challenge the status quo and embark on a transformative journey that would redefine leadership for the decades to come.

The persistent leadership gaps I faced were not mere obstacles; they were invitations to introspection and growth. As I stand at the threshold of this transformative journey, I carry with me the lessons learned from the early days of my career. The gaps illuminated the path forward, urging me to confront not only my shortcomings but also the systemic issues that hinder the collective progress of aspiring leaders.

In the following chapters, we will explore each leadership gap in greater detail, dissecting their challenges and unveiling the strategies to overcome them. This is not just a journey of personal development but a shared expedition towards a new era of leadership – one that values communication, embraces empathy, thrives on adaptability, and cherishes effective delegation.

As we navigate through the intricacies of leadership, let us remember that the gaps we encounter are not roadblocks but opportunities for growth. It is in acknowledging and addressing these gaps that we pave the way for a future where leadership is not just a title but a force that inspires, empowers, and transforms.

# Chapter 2:

# The Awakening

## Seeing the Light

In the early chapters of my career, as I eagerly embarked on the journey of leadership, little did I realize that pivotal moments awaited me—moments that would serve as profound wake-up calls, urging me to reevaluate and transform my leadership approach. These moments weren't just challenges; they were mirrors reflecting the gaps in my leadership style that needed urgent attention.

One such moment etched vividly in my memory unfolded during a high-pressure project. Deadlines loomed large, stress permeated the air, and the team grappled with the enormity of the task at hand. In the midst of this chaos, a glaring leadership gap emerged—the need for effective communication.

As the leader of the team, I bore the responsibility of ensuring clear communication. However, the lines of communication faltered, leaving the team adrift in confusion. It was a wake-up call, a realization that leadership wasn't merely about authority but about the art of conveying a vision in a way that resonates with each team member. This revelation set the stage for a transformative journey, compelling me to refine my communication skills and foster a collaborative environment.

But the journey of awakening didn't halt there. Another critical moment surfaced when a team member faced personal challenges affecting their performance. It was then that I confronted another leadership gap—the absence of empathy.

Amidst the pursuit of project milestones, I had inadvertently neglected the human side of leadership. True leadership, I realized, extends beyond task delegation; it demands an understanding of the individuals within the team. This wake-up call prompted a recalibration of my leadership compass, steering it toward a more compassionate and empathetic direction. The gap between professional expectations and personal well-being became a focal point, urging me to create an environment where team members felt seen, heard, and supported.

In the pursuit of refining my leadership style, I encountered a third wake-up call—an enlightening leadership seminar centered around Christ-centered principles. This experience uncovered another leadership gap—the need for spiritual grounding.

As the speaker expounded on the transformative power of Christ-centered leadership, I saw the profound impact that faith could have on the way we lead. True leadership, I realized, is about stewardship—of talents, responsibilities, and relationships. The gap between secular success and spiritual significance became evident, propelling me to integrate Christ-centered principles into my leadership style. This shift wasn't just professional; it represented a fundamental reorientation towards a higher purpose.

As I delved deeper into this Christ-centered approach, the fourth wake-up call materialized—the need for humility. The corporate world often celebrates confidence, but true leadership requires the humility to acknowledge our limitations. I had to confront the desire to always have the answers and instead embrace humility, seeking guidance, admitting mistakes, and fostering a culture of continuous learning.

These wake-up calls were more than just moments of recognition; they were catalysts for change, urging me to bridge the leadership gaps with a renewed sense of purpose and authenticity. The narrative of my early career isn't repetitive; it's a progression of self-discovery and transformation. Each wake-up call wasn't a roadblock but a stepping stone towards a more impactful and authentic leadership journey.

As we journey through the subsequent chapters, we will delve into each wake-up call, exploring the nuances of effective communication, empathy, spiritual grounding, and humility. This isn't just a recounting of past experiences; it's an invitation to embark on a shared exploration of leadership growth—a journey where each gap becomes an opportunity for development, and each wake-up call propels us toward becoming the leaders we are meant to be.

# Chapter 3:
# The Journey

Transitioning from a role as a Supervisor overseeing a team of 8-10 sales professionals to a Sales Manager leading 10-12 Sales Supervisors and their respective teams presented a significant shift in my leadership journey. During my initial week in this new position, I encountered the challenging task of terminating an associate's employment with the company. This situation was further complicated by the emotional investment the associate had developed since joining my team several months earlier when I was still in a supervisory role.

Upon first encountering this associate, I took the time to understand their motivations and goals. Despite not fitting the conventional mold of a successful salesperson, I recognized their potential and made it clear that achieving proficiency would require significant effort. The associate expressed commitment to this journey, and their determination was evident in their demeanor.

While the associate's initial performance fell slightly below the team average in the first month, we celebrated this achievement as it surpassed the performance of others in the fourth quartile. By the second month, the associate demonstrated significant improvement, reaching the floor's average in overall production.

This progress validated the efforts we had both invested in their development. However, my own career advancement to the role of Performance Coach, albeit brief, interrupted our collaborative efforts before I ascended to the role of Sales Manager.

Nearly three months later, I found myself in a meeting with the associate, confronting a drastic decline in their performance, placing them in the fourth quartile. It became clear during our conversation that our paths were diverging, and it was necessary to end their journey with the company. Despite anticipating this outcome, the associate's parting words resonated deeply with me and reignited my sense of purpose.

In expressing pride in my promotions and regret at the timing of our separation, the associate highlighted the impact of our brief collaboration on their development. Their acknowledgment of the positive trajectory under my guidance, followed by the subsequent decline, prompted me to reflect on my role in their journey and reinforced my commitment to my leadership mission.

The associate's candid feedback struck a chord, revealing a stark contrast between my leadership approach and that of others. They articulated a lack of care, concern, and interactive teaching style among previous leadership, emphasizing a deficiency in emotional intelligence, empathy, and encouragement.

Their heartfelt acknowledgment, coupled with tears, underscored the impact of genuine leadership on individual growth. Their assertion that such a conversation would not have occurred had I remained with them was both validating and sobering.

In that moment, I realized the imperative for our leadership team to embody the principles of "Servant Leadership" fully. Anything less would constitute a disservice to those we aim to support and develop. This realization ignited a fervent determination within me, shaping the mission I am committed to pursuing tirelessly.

Reflecting on my upbringing and experiences in sports, I recognized parallels between the growth process in leadership and excelling in athletics. This recognition led me to appreciate the universal laws at play, particularly the "Law of Gender," which underscores the necessity for nurturing and developing leadership qualities with patience and intentionality.

During my sales training journey, amidst the transition phase of handling live calls, I encountered a moment of uncertainty regarding a particular procedure. Seeking clarification and reassurance, I approached a sales coach with a question. However, the response I received was not what I anticipated. The coach's brief and seemingly dismissive reply left me feeling disheartened.

Despite the urge to react impulsively, I maintained composure and simply acknowledged their response.

This encounter, coupled with other challenging experiences detailed earlier in this chapter, left a lasting impression on me. It fueled my determination to evolve as a leader, particularly in adopting the principles of "Servant Leadership." My desire to spare others from similar experiences became a driving force for personal growth and development.

Recognizing the need to refine my communication skills, both verbal and non-verbal, became a focal point of my journey. I understood the importance of drawing from my own experiences, whether gleaned from sports or life's lessons, to inform my approach to leadership.

While my promotion to Sales Manager in late 2003 marked a significant milestone, the passing of my father in 2013 served as a catalyst for profound introspection and growth. His absence forced me to reevaluate my perspective on life and leadership.

Losing my father, who had become not only a parent but also a close friend and confidant, plunged me into a period of deep emotional turmoil. I grappled with feelings of anger and a sense of being robbed of future moments with him. Amidst this personal grief, I found myself confronted with well-intentioned yet seemingly automated condolences from others, which only served to exacerbate my frustration.

These experiences prompted me to confront the habitual nature of human interactions and the significance of genuine empathy. They served as a wake-up call, compelling me to reassess my own approach to connecting with others on a deeper, more authentic level.

A year prior, a member of my team faced the heart-wrenching experience of laying their 2-year-old child to rest. The gravity of this loss, compounded by the medical procedures and dashed hopes, weighed heavily on them. Following the funeral, this team member sought solace in my office, visibly distressed and expressing frustration at the well-meaning yet inadequate condolences offered by others.

Observing their pain, I couldn't help but question my own responses to such situations. It was reminiscent of my father's passing, prompting a moment of reflection on the unintended consequences of our ingrained social norms. These instances served as a wake-up call, propelling me towards a more deliberate path of personal growth.

Realizing the need for a shift in perspective, I recognized my duty not only to my own development but also to nurturing future leaders. This realization marked a pivotal moment in my journey, motivating me to adopt a more intentional approach to leadership and mentorship.

## Anecdotes & Insights

Growing up, my involvement in various sports, such as basketball, football, baseball, track, and tennis, provided me with invaluable insights into the parallels between athletic development and leadership growth. It dawned on me that these processes shared fundamental similarities, which I further connected with the Universal Laws, particularly the "Law of Gender."

The Law of Gender underscores the necessity for a gestation period for manifestation to occur. Just as a baby requires time in the womb and plants undergo their own periods of growth, ideas must be nurtured before they can materialize into tangible results. Understanding this law helped me recognize the importance of sowing seeds of intentionality to yield desired outcomes in both personal and professional endeavors.

Drawing from my athletic background, I reflected on the preparatory phases inherent in sports training. Whether through physical conditioning drills or mental preparation, the process of "prepping" was essential for peak performance. Marrying these ideologies together, I realized the significance of committing to a lifelong journey of intentional growth.

This realization served as a source of inspiration, driving me to embrace continuous evolution rather than stagnation. The cautionary tale of Blockbuster Video's failure to adapt to changing times serves as a poignant reminder of the consequences of complacency. It reinforced my commitment to remaining adaptable and resilient in the face of change, ensuring sustained personal and professional development.

## Challenges Faced

One of the hurdles I encountered on my journey was grappling with impatience and an inclination to rush the process. Like many, I found myself conditioned by the immediacy of technological advancements, which inadvertently skewed my perception of how quickly change should occur. The influence of conveniences like microwaves, virtual assistants, and GPS systems had subtly distorted my expectations.

In acknowledging this tendency, I chose to extend myself grace and recognize that personal development is a lifelong journey akin to the gradual progress observed in sports training. Embracing this perspective was a pivotal realization for me.

Moreover, as I cultivated self-compassion, I couldn't help but notice a similar gap in leadership practices among those I had encountered. Many leaders seemed to subscribe to the

"Microwaveable Society" mindset, expecting immediate results and overlooking the individualized nature of growth.

Understanding that everyone progresses at their own pace, I recognized the importance of fostering an environment of patience and empathy as a facilitator of growth. This realization led me to reflect on the leadership qualities exemplified by Christ Jesus, particularly his patience and dedication to ensuring his disciples truly understood his teachings.

Inspired by his approach, I began incorporating more analogies, metaphors, and storytelling techniques into my leadership style to bridge comprehension gaps. Additionally, I embraced the diversity of learning styles, acknowledging the need for flexibility in my methods of communication and development.

In essence, this journey served as a humbling reminder of the multifaceted nature of growth and the importance of embodying patience, empathy, and adaptability as both a leader and a learner.

## Resilience & Growth

I recall John Maxwell once sharing a thought that resonated deeply with me: that people often reach a point of change when the pain becomes unbearable. I liken this to what I refer to as "Popeye Moments," drawing inspiration from the beloved cartoon character Popeye.

In moments of adversity, Popeye would famously declare, "That's all I can stand, and I can't stand no more," before consuming his can of spinach. This simple act symbolized a surge of confidence and energy that propelled him forward.

Similarly, I view my life experiences as my own metaphorical spinach. Each success and failure has contributed to shaping my resilience and fortitude. Reflecting on these experiences has reinforced my belief in my ability to overcome challenges and inspired me to empower others to do the same.

This perspective has emboldened me to venture into uncharted territories of personal growth, drawing strength from my resilience. As a supervisor, I even introduced cans of spinach to my sales team as a daily reminder of the power of resilience in facing obstacles.

By fostering an environment that embraces resilience and growth, I aim to instill in others the confidence to persevere and thrive in the face of adversity.

I recall instances where my skin color became an obstacle for some individuals, who expressed discomfort working with me because of it. This was not a misinterpretation, as it was explicitly stated by an associate that they were uncomfortable working with a Black man.

While these experiences were hurtful, they echoed memories from my teenage years in New York City, where I encountered similar biases from individuals of different racial backgrounds. Despite the pain, I had anticipated such situations based on past events, and I drew upon my resilience to navigate through them.

As the only Black male leadership member at the time, I realized I was forging a path for others. This realization was underscored during a heartfelt conversation with Nate Smith, a Sales Supervisor on my team.

I choose to view these challenges as opportunities for personal growth, recognizing that God was shaping me through adversity. Reflecting on the biblical verse Romans 8:31, I found solace in the belief that divine purpose transcends individual circumstances.

Despite facing unwarranted attacks on my character and directives, I reached a breaking point. Nate's intervention served as a wake-up call. He reminded me of the significance of my position as the first and only Black male leader in the region, emphasizing the importance of my actions in shaping perceptions and paving the way for others.

Upon hearing Nate's words, despite standing tall at 6'1", I felt as though I had shrunk to a mere inch in height. His message hit me with such force that tears threatened to spill, but I held them back, confronted by the undeniable truth he spoke.

Nate's words served as a stark reminder of the impact my actions and decisions could have on those around me, particularly those who looked up to me as a leader. He challenged me to consider the message I would convey by giving up, highlighting the importance of perseverance and resilience in paving the way for others.

At that moment, I reached for my metaphorical can of spinach once again, drawing upon my inner strength and resolve. Nate's words became a catalyst for transformation, empowering me to confront challenges head-on with unwavering determination.

Reflecting on this experience, I am reminded of the mysterious ways in which divine intervention operates. I am a firm believer that everything happens for a reason and that God allows us to face trials to impart valuable lessons that we may have overlooked in less painful circumstances.

The growth process is indeed a journey filled with ups and downs, often accompanied by discomfort and challenges. However, it is through embracing resilience that we emerge stronger and more equipped to navigate life's obstacles.

This experience marked a pivotal moment in my journey toward maturity and growth as a servant leader. It reinforced the notion that not everyone may understand or accept our paths, but it is our resilience and steadfastness in our beliefs that define us.

## Painting a Vivid Picture

In my journey of transformation, I recognized the need to reprogram my mindset; as Mark Twain astutely observed, education often begins with unlearning what we've been taught. This process required delving into the underlying reasons behind human behavior and speech patterns and understanding that our actions and words are often shaped by conditioning from our upbringing, social circles, and broader societal influences.

I embarked on a deep exploration of how the brain functions, particularly the distinction between the subconscious and conscious mind. Understanding that our subconscious stores every experience we encounter, often leading us to operate on autopilot, was a profound revelation. Conversely, our conscious mind allows for more intentional and purposeful decision-making, albeit within a limited timeframe.

I delved into the intricacies of brain anatomy and function, exploring topics such as the different brain lobes, the dichotomy between the left and right hemispheres, and the stages of brain development from infancy to adulthood. This knowledge enabled me to grasp the optimal timing for reprogramming oneself, tapping into various brainwave states from delta to beta.

Additionally, I integrated exercise into my study of brain function, recognizing its profound effects on stress reduction and the release of hormones and chemicals that promote feelings of well-being and enhance cognitive function. The synergy between physical activity and mental clarity was a powerful revelation that continues to resonate with me.

Overall, this journey of self-discovery and reprogramming has been transformative and continues to shape my understanding of human behavior, cognitive processes, and personal growth.

## Reflection

Reflecting on this chapter of my life, I am reminded of the pain endured on the path of growth and the weighty responsibilities of servant leadership. It's a sobering truth that we all possess inner strength, akin to Popeye's can of spinach, yet often fail to tap into it when faced with adversity.

I want readers to understand the power of leveraging their own reservoirs of resilience. By embracing these truths, one can cultivate a sense of momentum toward becoming a better version of themselves. This intentional journey fosters both self-discovery and awareness, paving the way for unexpected successes.

Henry David Thoreau's words resonate deeply with this sentiment: "If one advances confidently in the direction of his dreams and endeavors to live the life which he has imagined, he will meet with a success unexpected in common hours." This quote serves as a poignant reminder of the transformative power of determination and authenticity in pursuing one's aspirations.

## Future Directions

In the forthcoming chapters, I intend to delve deeper into the individual components of TMC (TEACH, MODEL, COACH), exploring various stages of my personal transformation. These chapters will provide a more comprehensive understanding of the journey I embarked upon and the insights gained along the way. Stay tuned as we explore the intricacies of each component and the profound impact they have had on my growth and development.

# Chapter 4:
# The Pay-Off

In the Teach, Model, and Coach methodology, the foundational principles serve as a platform for fostering genuine connections in a world dominated by business and technology. Effective leadership hinges on adept communication, recognizing that true connection begins with active listening and valuing others' perspectives. This emphasis on valuing individuals fosters stronger relationships and deeper engagement.

Reflecting on shared experiences and personal journeys, a common thread emerges the importance of clear and specific communication that leaves others feeling respected, engaged, and uplifted. These principles form the bedrock of the Teach, Model, and Coach model. When expectations are clearly communicated, and individuals understand the initiative, they are better equipped to contribute effectively, resulting in a synergistic environment that yields results.

Moreover, modeling provides tangible examples of success, reducing ambiguity and instilling confidence in individuals. Even in instances where mistakes occur, an environment centered on equipping individuals with specific coaching and guidance, coupled with encouragement and empowerment, fosters inspiration and long-term sustainability.

Motivation may serve as a temporary catalyst, but true sustainability is achieved through inspiration, which ignites a deeper sense of purpose and commitment. The Teach, Model, and Coach approach is built upon these enduring attributes, encouraging individuals to align with their intrinsic motivations and recognize the collective impact of their efforts on organizational success.

As we delve deeper into the Teach, Model, and Coach methodology in subsequent chapters, we will explore practical strategies for implementation and further insights into cultivating a culture of empowerment, growth, and sustainability. Stay tuned for a deeper exploration of these transformative principles.

## Methodology's Tangible Results:

In my role as a Sales Supervisor, I had the privilege of guiding, motivating, and empowering my team to remarkable heights, transforming us from the 22nd-ranked team on the sales floor to the top-ranking team within a year. Our collective achievements were unprecedented, setting new company-wide records and making a resounding statement as a cohesive unit. My strength lies in my ability to work closely with each sales professional, providing personalized support and guidance.

Transitioning to the role of Sales Manager presented a unique set of challenges, requiring a shift in mindset and approach. It was a humbling experience that necessitated relinquishing control and adopting a more empowering leadership style. Like a compassionate drill sergeant in boot camp, I recognized the importance of fostering a culture of trust, patience, and passion for the development of my team members. This transformation didn't come easily, but each lesson learned along the way contributed to my growth as a leader.

Following the passing of my father in 2013, I embarked on a deliberate journey of self-improvement, seeking to become a more effective leader. Attending a John Maxwell certification conference in 2016 sparked the inception of the Teach, Model, and Coach methodology. It wasn't until 2017 that I began implementing this new approach, and by the summer of 2018, the results were undeniable. My team's outstanding performance catapulted us to the top spot nationwide in sales, marking a significant milestone in my career. Despite having served as a Sales Manager since 2003, achieving a company-wide number-one ranking had eluded me until July of 2018.

I vividly recall the moment of celebration when my team members surprised me during a meeting with #1 balloons and cupcakes, commemorating our remarkable achievement. It was a testament to the power of collaboration, determination, and effective leadership. As I continue on my journey, I am committed to further refining the Teach, Model, and Coach methodology and empowering others to reach their full potential.

While I wasn't actively seeking recognition, it became abundantly clear that my team was laser-focused on surpassing their peers in key performance metrics such as sales, closure rates, quality, and ancillary product offerings. Witnessing their dedication and drive filled me with immense pride, prompting me to shower them with praise and appreciation during our team meeting. It was truly remarkable to achieve the top spot companywide amidst stiff competition from numerous Sales Managers, supervisors, and sales professionals.

But the story doesn't end there. The following month, in August 2018, my team replicated their success by once again clinching the coveted number-one position across the company. This consecutive feat was nothing short of extraordinary, and I made sure to express my admiration and support to each member of the team. With each achievement, I witnessed a tangible increase in their confidence and a deeper sense of value and purpose.

As if that weren't enough, the momentum continued into September, my birthday month, with yet another remarkable achievement. This time, my team secured the top spot for the third consecutive month, solidifying their status as the best-performing team in the company. I commend each member—Shana, David, Kayla, Mike, Debbie, JB, Jose, Jamal, and Dan—for their unwavering dedication and contribution to our collective success.

Throughout 2018, our team consistently ranked in the top quartile companywide, a testament to our commitment to excellence and collaboration. Despite changes in team composition, I was inspired by how seamlessly new team members embraced their roles and supported their peers. Our culture thrived on community, with everyone looking out for one another's success.

I fondly referred to our team as the "Bad Boy" side, drawing parallels to the groundbreaking era of Puff Daddy and Bad Boy Records in the mid-90s. Much like the innovative spirit of that era, my team approached their work with an authentic swagger, setting new standards and pushing boundaries with each achievement.

In 2019, our team continued to shine, securing the top ranking an impressive five times throughout the year. However, the onset of 2020 brought unforeseen challenges as we transitioned to remote work—a path unfamiliar to all of us. Despite the initial adjustments, we adapted swiftly and maintained our position at the pinnacle, achieving the number one ranking three times and consistently placing in the top quartile companywide.

The year 2021 proved to be our crowning achievement as we clinched the prestigious title of the number one team overall for the entire year. This remarkable success was a testament to our unwavering dedication and resilience in the face of adversity.

As we entered 2022, our streak of excellence continued, with our team maintaining the number one ranking companywide for nearly 18 consecutive months. This sustained level of performance is undoubtedly a noteworthy accomplishment, reflecting our relentless commitment to excellence and teamwork.

## Impact of the Approach:

The implementation of the Teach, Model, and Coach approach had a profound impact on the dynamics within my team, fostering a deeper sense of connection and camaraderie akin to that of a family. Witnessing their collective growth was immensely rewarding, particularly as I observed a noticeable increase in teamwork and mutual support among team members—a development that pleasantly surprised me.

One of the most gratifying outcomes was the heightened level of ownership displayed by each team member. Previously, I often found myself extinguishing multiple fires on a weekly basis, but now, they have embraced a proactive approach, making executive decisions and taking responsibility for their actions. This shift underscored the effectiveness of our empowerment and development efforts, leaving me reassured and proud of their progress.

What truly struck me was the sense of confidence and self-sufficiency they exhibited, especially in my absence during meetings or vacations. Knowing that the team could adeptly handle any situation without my direct involvement was a testament to their growth and the success of our collaborative efforts.

I have a vivid memory of a cherished mentor, Michelle Trindade, imparting invaluable wisdom to me. She said, "T, aim to work yourself out of a job so that when you're not present, your team can execute with the same level of proficiency." These words resonated deeply with me, serving as a powerful affirmation of the effectiveness of my Teach, Model, and Coach methodology.

## Presentation of Facts and Anecdotes:

Throughout the journey of nurturing my team's development, I found great value in understanding the underlying "why" behind their actions and aspirations. By delving into personal insights and recognizing their individual triggers and motivations, I was able to tailor my approach to each team member, fostering a deeper connection and understanding.

During our interactions, I often paused to provide real-time examples of the growth process, highlighting key moments where I demonstrated the principles we were discussing. This hands-on approach not only solidified the learning experience but also sparked moments of enlightenment for my team members as they began to grasp the concepts on a deeper level.

Drawing inspiration from a phrase I encountered in a Dallas Cowboys sports series, "You get what you demand, and you encourage what you tolerate," I adopted it as a guiding mantra for our team. This phrase encapsulated the essence of our leadership philosophy, emphasizing the importance of setting high standards and holding ourselves accountable while also nurturing an environment that promotes growth and excellence over complacency.

I distinctly remember the moments when my team members would seek solace in my office, closing the door behind them and taking a seat to share their challenges. As they poured out their frustrations, I listened attentively, allowing them the space to express themselves fully.

In these moments, it was common for them to simply vent their feelings without posing any specific questions. With a gentle touch of humor, I would acknowledge their concerns and then gently redirect the conversation by asking if there was a specific question they wanted to address.

Their frustration was palpable, yet endearing, as I witnessed their growth unfold before me in real-time. When they inevitably asked for my advice, I would turn the question back to them, encouraging them to reflect on their own thoughts and instincts. This approach initially met with resistance from my team members, as it challenged them to think independently and take ownership of their decisions.

It became apparent to me that many of my team members were products of what I termed a "microwaveable society." Instant gratification was the norm, with answers readily available at the push of a button from Siri, Alexa, or Google. This reliance on technology was impeding their personal growth, leading to a sense of complacency that needed to be addressed.

Breaking free from this cycle of dependency was essential for their development, and it required a concerted effort to challenge their comfort zones. Gradually, they began to embrace the process and experience significant growth. After each learning session, I would reinforce this with a simple yet powerful reminder: "You get what you demand, and you encourage what you tolerate." This served as a wake-up call, highlighting the importance of setting high standards and refusing to settle for mediocrity.

Witnessing the transformation unfold was truly gratifying. Over time, I observed my team members internalizing this mantra, incorporating it into their daily lives with the same ease as reciting their own names. It was a testament to the effectiveness of the Teach, Model, and Coach approach, instilling valuable lessons that resonated deeply with each individual.

## Conclusion and Call to Action:

Unfortunately, despite the impactful strides made in leadership development on the "Bad Boy" side of the house, it became apparent that there was a noticeable gap within our organization as a whole. While our team flourished with the Teach, Model, and Coach methodology, there remained significant deficiencies in leadership maturity across the board.

Addressing this gap proved to be a challenging uphill battle, as the traditional approaches to leadership development fell short in fostering true growth and empowerment. While initiatives such as projects, reports analysis, and diversity training have their merits, they often overlook the fundamental skills needed for effective leadership.

True leadership development goes beyond mere technical competencies, emphasizing the ability to communicate effectively, inspire others, and cultivate a culture of mentorship and growth.

Unfortunately, many corporate settings fall short in this regard, relying on stale and robotic methods that lack emotional intelligence.

As a result, associates are left feeling disengaged and stressed, hindering productivity and overall organizational success. Recognizing this pressing need for change, it became my mission to advocate for a more holistic approach to leadership development, one that prioritizes human connection and empowerment at every level.

Imagine a world where every leader is effectively equipped with the Teach, Model, and Coach methodology. The ripple effects of such a transformation would be profound, extending far beyond the workplace.

With leaders who prioritize communication, inspiration, and mentorship, organizations would experience greater associate retention, increased productivity, and a heightened sense of value among team members. These positive outcomes would not only enhance the work environment but also enrich the lives of employees outside of work.

In households across the globe, the benefits would be equally impactful. Improved communication skills, patience, and grace cultivated in the workplace would translate into stronger relationships and more harmonious family dynamics.

The impact of the TMC methodology was powerfully demonstrated during my retirement gathering in February 2023. As attendees shared their testimonies, it became clear how deeply they felt valued and cared for under this leadership approach. These heartfelt reflections were captured in episodes 22 and 23 of my "Leadership Reflections" video series, underscoring the urgency of spreading this methodology far and wide to make a tangible difference in people's lives. It's time to ensure that every leader has the tools to foster positive change, both within their organizations and beyond.

## Building on the Foundation:

The narrative unfolds like a captivating story, weaving seamlessly between past and present, revealing the ongoing journey of growth and discovery. At its core lies a recurring theme: the recognition of gaps in leadership and the relentless pursuit of growth within those gaps.

As the story unfolds, the reader is transported back in time to pivotal moments of reflection and realization. Memories of challenges faced and lessons learned resurface, offering valuable insights into the evolution of leadership philosophy.

With each flashback, the reader gains a deeper understanding of the protagonist's transformation. From the early days of uncertainty and self-discovery to the present-day achievements and milestones, the narrative paints a vivid picture of growth and resilience.

Throughout the narrative, the theme of identifying and addressing leadership gaps remains constant. The protagonist's journey is marked by a commitment to continuous improvement and a willingness to confront challenges head-on.

As the story progresses, the reader is drawn into the protagonist's world, experiencing the highs and lows of leadership firsthand. Moments of triumph and moments of struggle are intertwined, creating a dynamic narrative arc that keeps the reader engaged from beginning to end.

Ultimately, the story serves as a testament to the power of self-reflection, growth, and perseverance. It is a reminder that true leadership is not about perfection but about the willingness to learn, adapt, and grow in the face of adversity. And as the protagonist's journey demonstrates, the path to becoming a better leader is a journey worth taking, no matter how challenging it may be.

## Reflection on the Methodology:

Looking back on the Teach, Model, and Coach (TMC) approach, I realize that for far too long, I allowed societal norms to shape my perception of leadership, and I, like many others, missed the mark significantly. Even in my days as an athlete, I experienced coaching styles that were characterized by demoralizing tactics such as yelling, insults, and devaluation. Sadly, this behavior was not only accepted but expected in the sports environment.

Regrettably, this toxic leadership culture permeated into the corporate world, where it became ingrained as the norm. Despite experiencing firsthand the detrimental effects of such leadership practices, many leaders remained entrenched in the mindset of "we've always done it this way," stifling any potential for growth. This resistance to change is reminiscent of Blockbuster Video's downfall, as they clung stubbornly to outdated ideologies, ultimately leading to their demise.

My own awakening to the shortcomings of traditional leadership methods inspired me to adopt the TMC approach. I vowed to make a difference by breaking away from the status quo and implementing a more empowering and effective leadership style. By embracing TMC, I sought to create a culture where every individual felt valued, respected, and empowered to reach their full potential.

In essence, TMC represented a paradigm shift—a departure from the outdated and ineffective leadership models of the past toward a more progressive and impactful approach. It was a recognition that true leadership is about nurturing and empowering others rather than exerting control or instilling fear.

As I look back on this transformative journey, I am reminded of the importance of challenging conventional wisdom and being willing to embrace change. By daring to challenge the norms and adopt a more enlightened approach to leadership, I not only transformed my own leadership style but also created a ripple effect that resonated throughout my team and beyond.

Effective leadership and mentorship are grounded in trust. When leaders fail to align their words with their actions, trust is eroded. The Teach, Model, and Coach (TMC) methodology emphasizes the importance of integrity and consistency in leadership. Leaders are taught to uphold their commitments and demonstrate authenticity in their interactions. By prioritizing the needs and development of those they lead, TMC embodies the principles of servant leadership and mentoring.

In TMC, leaders are encouraged to make their agenda synonymous with the growth and success of their team members. This approach fosters a culture of trust where individuals feel supported and valued. By leading with honesty and transparency, TMC practitioners inspire confidence and loyalty among their team members. Ultimately, true leadership and mentorship are characterized by a commitment to authenticity and a genuine dedication to the well-being and advancement of others.

## Broader Audience Engagement:

I anticipate that individuals will be motivated to engage in further exploration of these principles and their implementation in their respective environments. While I haven't provided detailed guidance on integrating these practices into other settings, I am fully capable of doing so.

# Chapter 5:

# TEACH

## The Foundation of Servant Leadership

Early on in my life, I encountered a big communication problem that's like a cancer in our society: "assumption." When I played sports, my coaches often tried to teach us things, assuming we were all on the same page. But many times, we weren't. This caused frustration for both the coach and us players. Some of us started feeling disconnected from the coach because he'd get emotionally abusive when we didn't understand. But because we were athletes, we felt like we had to tough it out and deal with it.

Sadly, I've seen this same unhealthy behavior in the corporate world, too. It really devalues people and creates division and distrust. I even caught myself doing it before I realized how damaging it was. That was when I decided to change my approach to communication.

I remember a time when I lost my cool and publicly yelled at a colleague, demanding they get back to work because we were busy. At that moment, I was so focused on meeting targets and handling incoming calls that I didn't think about how my behavior was affecting others. I didn't realize the impact it had on not just that one colleague but on the whole team who saw it happen. Who would want to give their best for a leader who belittles and yells at them? It was definitely not a good look, and I knew I had to make a change.

The impact of my actions became clear when I found out that a colleague had filed a letter of concern with our regional president, someone I deeply admire, Mr. George Rogers. I was called into George's office, not expecting to discuss what had happened. Walking in with my usual carefree attitude, I was hit with reality.

George handled the situation gracefully. He calmly explained why I was there, mentioning the associate's concern, and then asked for my side of the story. It wasn't an interrogation; it felt more like he was gathering information for a news report. Once he understood what had occurred, he leaned back and asked me to consider how the colleague might have felt being publicly criticized. He urged me to imagine the emotions they might have experienced, suggesting that past traumas could have been triggered.

It was a wake-up call for me. George's approach made me realize the deeper impact of my actions. I hadn't thought about how my behavior could reopen old wounds for someone else. It was a moment of reflection, understanding the importance of empathy and how our actions can affect others in ways we might not immediately see.

From that day on, I made a commitment to approach situations with more sensitivity and awareness. I learned to pause and consider the feelings of those around me before reacting impulsively. George's guidance helped me grow not only as a professional but also as a person, teaching me the value of empathy and understanding in communication.

These were thoughts I never considered before, especially in the heat of the moment. Back then, all I cared about was getting those phones answered and making sales.

But then George did something unexpected. He asked me to imagine how the colleague must have felt emotionally. Suddenly, I saw things from their perspective. I felt the pain and disappointment I might have caused them, and the thought of letting George down hit me hard.

What really struck me was when George said, "Troy, you're capable of so much more. When you look back on this, what could you have done differently?" That made me pause and really think. I remembered a metaphor I once heard about radio stations: WII-FM, which stands for "What's In It For Me." I realized that if I had taken the time to explain the situation clearly, highlighting its importance and how it would benefit everyone involved—the colleague, the customer, and the company—it could have been a win-win for all. It was like a lightbulb went off in my head.

George nodded in agreement and said, "That's the Troy I know. You have so much potential, and that behavior doesn't reflect who you truly are. We need you to consistently bring your best self to the table. That's when we all succeed."

From that conversation, I felt the impact of the power of empathy and clear communication. I realized that taking a moment to consider others' perspectives and communicating effectively can make a huge difference in any situation. It was a turning point for me, and I made a commitment to show up as the best version of myself, just like George believed I could.

He was absolutely right, and throughout our conversation, he showed me immense value and appreciation. His words carried a powerful tone that motivated me to make things right for the mistake I had made. I told George that I intended to apologize not only to the associate directly involved but to all those who witnessed the incident.

With a smile and a nod, George acknowledged my decision as a step towards greater leadership. As I embarked on apologizing to everyone involved, George leaned in and affirmed that I was one of his top leaders. However, he emphasized that such incidents could never occur again and encouraged me to continue growing and maintaining consistency and discipline in my leadership approach. It was a pivotal moment for me as George demonstrated how to communicate effectively while also teaching, guiding, and allowing me to rewrite the narrative of what had transpired.

This experience marked the beginning of a new chapter, focusing on the first pillar of effective leadership: Teaching. A vital aspect of leadership is engaging in communication that uplifts and values individuals rather than disconnecting or devaluing them. This foundation is essential because effective leadership cannot exist without it. We delve into strategies for becoming a more effective and impactful communicator, emphasizing clarity, storytelling, and transparency. Additionally, we recognize the importance of avoiding actions that may emotionally harm or trigger others, striving to value people in every communication opportunity. It's about building a culture where every interaction honors and respects individuals.

## Teaching as a Foundational Element:

I came across an insightful article by Vanessa Boris on The Harvard Business Publishing Corporate Learning Blog. She talked about how stories play a significant role in conveying culture, history, and values, bringing people together and giving them a shared sense of identity. This resonated with me deeply as I reflected on my own experiences.

Boris emphasized how storytelling strengthens the bond within organizations by creating connections and engaging various types of learners. Stories have a unique ability to stick in our minds because they relate to our own relationships and life experiences. This makes the content more relatable and meaningful.

**(Source):**

The Harvard Business Publishing Corporate Learning Blog

December 20, 2017 by Vanessa Boris

## Personal Stories:

As I wrapped up my first year as a sales supervisor, I couldn't help but feel proud of my team's incredible progress. When I took on the role in November 2001, we were ranked second to last out of 23 teams on the sales floor. But by December, we had climbed to the top spot, breaking records along the way. It was an amazing achievement, and we were all basking in the glory of our success.

Just when things were looking up, my mentor and friend, Michelle Trindade, dropped a bombshell. She informed me that I had been chosen to chair our philanthropy team. Initially, I hesitated. The thought of being away from my team for meetings, events, and other responsibilities didn't appeal to me. So, I respectfully declined the offer.

Michelle was taken aback by my refusal. She explained that I had been specifically requested for this opportunity, but I still couldn't see the immediate value in it. Undeterred, she informed me that I would need to explain my decision to our regional president, George.

Although I felt confident in my decision, I knew I had to face George and explain my reasoning. I didn't feel scared or intimidated; I was ready to stand by my choice.

This experience taught me the importance of staying true to my priorities and values, even in the face of unexpected opportunities. It also showed me the value of open communication and being able to confidently express my decisions to others, regardless of their position.

During our meeting, I felt confident using a sports analogy because I knew George was a fan, just like me. I started by telling George about a rookie outfielder who had an outstanding first year, winning awards like "Rookie of the Year" and league MVP. Now, the organization wanted to move him to play 3rd base, a position he wasn't used to. I explained how this change could hurt the team rather than strengthen it.

George listened with interest, nodding along as I spoke. Then, he leaned back in his chair and shared his own experience. He told me that he had also played outfield and was once asked to switch to 3rd base. He called it "the hot corner" because the balls come at you much faster and often take unpredictable bounces. He described how it could leave you with marks, bruises, and aches.

But despite the challenges, George explained, you learn to adapt to the position. He said that true all-stars shine no matter where they play on the field. They have that special "it" factor that sets them apart.

This conversation with George taught me a valuable lesson about resilience and adaptability. Just like in sports, in life and work, we sometimes find ourselves in unfamiliar positions. But with determination and the right mindset, we can overcome any challenge and continue to excel. It's about embracing change and trusting in our abilities to thrive in any situation.

During our conversation, George asked me about my aspirations to become a sales manager. I told him I envisioned reaching that level within five years. But George disagreed; he believed I had the potential to achieve it much sooner. He explained that taking on the role of Chairperson would enhance my multitasking skills, ability to develop others, and maintain excellent results—all essential qualities of an effective manager.

He emphasized that growth opportunities like this one were crucial for personal and professional development. George couldn't force anyone to seize such chances, but he encouraged me to think it over and give him my decision the following Monday.

Leaving that meeting, I felt both challenged and inspired. Despite standing tall at 6'1", I felt as though I'd shrunk to just 1" in height. However, I made the decision to accept the Chairperson opportunity. I threw myself into the role, managing it successfully alongside other responsibilities and supporting my team.

Remarkably, just ten months later, I was promoted to sales manager—a testament to the effectiveness of George's guidance and encouragement.

What struck me most was how George tailored his approach to motivate and inspire me. By taking the analogy I initiated and customizing it to resonate with me, he demonstrated a deep understanding of who I am and how to bring out my best. This experience taught me the importance of adapting my communication style to suit different audiences and recipients—a valuable skill I continue to develop. George's approach was not only effective but also empowering, showing me the impact of personalized motivation and encouragement in achieving success.

George's approach made it clear to me that the decision was a no-brainer. He highlighted the valuable insights gained from recognizing the challenges of growth.

Understanding why my team members come to work and what inspires and motivates them became crucial. Building strong relationships ensures that my actions consistently reflect their value to me. It's about acknowledging their importance and supporting their growth.

## Transformative Power of Imparting Knowledge:

Understanding the "why" behind our actions is essential for leaders. It builds trust with our team members. When you can explain the reasons behind directives, it strengthens the connection and clarity in communication. If you're unsure of the "why," don't hesitate to ask questions before giving directions.

Another key is tuning into your team's WII-FM station: "What's In It For Me." Recognizing their interests helps tailor your message to engage them effectively. By consistently communicating the "whys" behind decisions and setting clear expectations, I saw a significant boost in trust from my team.

I found that using the "what, when, where, and how" approach enhanced communication further. Clearly defining the initiative (what) and explaining its importance sets the stage. Showing implementation dates (when) gives a tangible timeline for results. Focusing on areas needing improvement (where) clarifies the path forward. Finally, detailing the game plan (how) ensures everyone understands the process from start to finish without any gaps. This approach led to smoother execution and better outcomes.

One of the toughest parts of my journey towards growth was learning to be patient, both with myself and my team. It often felt like a comedy show because many team members wanted quick fixes to their problems. I used to give in and provide instant solutions, thinking it would help. But I realized it was actually hindering our progress in the long run.

I needed to break this cycle by consistently teaching and developing my team to become leaders themselves. This process, inspired by my mentor Micelle Trindade, was about multiplying my impact and eventually working myself out of a job.

As I committed to this path, I noticed my team members observing and learning from my actions in real-time. This became a valuable reference point for their own growth. I even jokingly called the office my "communication growth playground" because of how much I practiced there.

But what amazed me most was how these principles extended beyond work and into my personal life. I found myself applying the same patience and teaching methods outside of the office, seeing positive results in all areas of my life. It was a powerful reminder of the impact of consistent effort and dedication to personal development.

## Cultivating Team Growth and Development:

When it came to nurturing the growth and development of my team, I leaned on a strategy I had already used: "Get To Know You Sessions." These were one-on-one meetings where I delved deep into understanding each team member's "why." We talked about their families, dreams, and standards and even touched on personal struggles and growth.

These sessions required me to lead by example, being open and transparent about my own experiences. I shared my professional aspirations and the journey I was on. It was about building genuine trust. My team could see that I was authentic and honest with them. And when I made mistakes, I didn't shy away—I owned up to them and shared the lessons I learned.

I wanted my team to understand that we're all constantly learning and growing in life. By being real with them, I earned their trust and respect. They saw me as someone they could trust, and they were inspired to follow my lead in their own personal and professional journeys.

This approach wasn't just about building a team—it was about creating a culture of honesty, vulnerability, and continuous growth. And as my team bought into this leadership style, they began to embody it themselves, fostering a community of support and progress.

In my journey of leadership, I made sure to empower my team by assigning them various responsibilities. Sometimes, I let them volunteer, and other times, I chose based on specific criteria. When I selected someone, I made sure to explain why I picked them and how I believed this responsibility would contribute to their personal growth journey. This approach worked well for most of them, as the trust we had built allowed for effective collaboration.

However, there were a few instances where the added responsibility became overwhelming for developing leaders. In those cases, I prioritized their well-being and removed the burden from their shoulders. I remembered George Rogers' advice about not forcing people into growth opportunities and respecting their feelings and needs during that time. This approach further strengthened the trust within our team.

I also measured their success through metrics and the results their teams achieved. This provided tangible evidence of how they were implementing their learnings and strategies. By consistently modeling and developing them, I saw their growth reflected in their results.

This approach wasn't just about achieving numbers—it was about fostering a culture of trust, support, and continuous improvement. As my team embraced their responsibilities and learned from their experiences, they grew not only as individuals but also as effective leaders.

In my journey of guiding my team's growth, I found a powerful method to gauge their enthusiasm and hunger for learning. During our staff meetings, I would select one team member to lead the discussion. I would demonstrate how to lead effectively, explaining the reasons behind certain questions and empowering them to dive even deeper, especially when addressing challenging metrics.

This approach resonated with them because it showed that I wasn't just critiquing their performance but genuinely investing in their development. They appreciated the opportunity to take the lead and rotate this responsibility amongst themselves, giving them time to prepare and contribute meaningfully. It was gratifying to witness their growth, and this practice proved invaluable whenever I was away from the office.

Moreover, some team members showed exceptional eagerness to learn. They would approach me with a notepad, seeking guidance on particularly challenging scenarios. This demonstrated their dedication and reinforced the effectiveness of my approach. I seized these opportunities to provide personalized mentorship, recognizing the unique needs of each individual.

However, I must admit I didn't always get it right. There were times when my approach fell short, but I learned from these experiences. Through trial and error, I discovered the importance of customizing my approach to ensure every team member felt valued and could benefit from my guidance. It was a continuous journey of refinement and growth, but seeing the positive impact on my team made it all worthwhile.

## Connection to Servant Leadership Principles:

In the foundation of teaching and guiding your team, the key is to focus on their needs, aspirations, and dreams. As a leader, your goal should be to empower them to pursue and achieve their "whys." It starts with truly listening to their desires and then working collaboratively to help them attain their objectives. The ultimate agenda for a leader should be to unlock the full potential of each team member, leading them toward their own version of success.

However, life is unpredictable, and challenges outside of work can arise. Whether it's personal struggles, the loss of loved ones, or relationship difficulties, these issues can profoundly impact your team members. As a leader, it's crucial to show genuine empathy and support during these times. When you say, "I've got you," it's essential to follow through and demonstrate your commitment to their well-being.

Living in Florida, I often encouraged my team members to take a trip to the beach for relaxation and rejuvenation. I would suggest they go during work hours, emphasizing that their well-being is a priority. I shared my own experiences of finding solace and peace at the beach, hoping they could also benefit from its beauty and serenity. Of course, I made sure to suggest alternatives for those who didn't enjoy the beach. The key was to encourage healthy escapes that suited each individual's preferences. This is what true support looks like under the principles of servant leadership—prioritizing the well-being and growth of your team members above all else.

I introduced my team to the powerful concepts of family and community, taking our teamwork to new heights. It became more than just working together—it was about intentional connection and building personal bonds. This sense of identity resonated deeply with them, and one team member even likened my leadership style to that of Bad Boy records, which stuck with everyone. We embraced this identity and became the "Bad Boy" family on our sales floor, embodying a unique swagger in everything we did, from our attire to our lifestyles outside of work: work hard, play hard, love harder.

When I transitioned to Sales Training Manager, I carried this concept forward, creating a community where new hires were nurtured and supported. Within this community, everyone looked out for each other, fostering a sense of collective responsibility. I often referred to the results of this approach as our "body of work." When people feel valued and supported, it boosts productivity, reduces turnover, and cultivates a culture of mutual respect and appreciation.

By prioritizing connection and creating a sense of belonging, we were able to build a strong and cohesive team environment. This sense of unity propelled us to greater heights and ensured that every team member felt seen, heard, and valued.

In the Teach foundation, I placed significant emphasis on the dangers of assumptions in communication. I demonstrated how easily we fall into the trap of assuming instead of truly understanding. Often, we hear a question or request and immediately jump to conclusions without probing deeper or seeking clarification. However, effective listening requires us to dig deeper to uncover the true needs or intentions behind the communication. When we take the time to do this, we foster greater trust and appreciation in our relationships.

This principle is especially crucial when teaching new concepts. We should never assume that others already know what we're teaching. Instead, we should provide clear, detailed explanations and guidance, ensuring that we address specifics and provide step-by-step instructions. It's essential to circle back and check for understanding, confirming that our team members have truly absorbed the information. By doing so, we demonstrate our value and commitment to their growth and development.

# Integration of Personal and Leadership Development:

I've often heard the saying, "success leaves clues," and upon reflection, I've found it to be undeniably true. When I look back on areas of my life where I've experienced success, I can see the patterns and clues that led me there. However, it wasn't always smooth sailing. There were times of struggle and challenge when I had to endure growing pains.

During those moments of growth, it often felt like I was in the dark, unsure of why I was facing such difficulties. But looking back now, I realize that those challenges were shaping me into a stronger and more resilient leader. The phrase "no pain, no gain" took on a deeper meaning for me as I understood the value of the growth I received, even when it seemed overwhelming.

Now, I can share those experiences with other leaders I mentor. I provide them with insight into the weight of the challenges they face and offer credibility by sharing my own journey of growth and transformation. It's akin to respecting the process, much like in sports, where discipline and perseverance are essential for success.

Reflecting on my journey, I understand the importance of remembering the lessons learned along the way. While challenges may seem daunting at the moment, they ultimately contribute to our growth and development as leaders. It's about embracing the process and trusting that each obstacle we overcome brings us one step closer to achieving our goals.

Facts are the experiences and lessons I've already lived through and grown from. They're the disciplines I've acquired and the attributes I've developed over time. Now, as I embark on new endeavors, I recognize the value of these facts and channel their energy into my current pursuits.

I often remind others that these facts don't have to come from sports; they can stem from any past experience where one has overcome challenges and gained valuable insights. It's about tapping into the effort, energy, and knowledge gained from those experiences to tackle present obstacles.

However, it's common for people to forget their own facts, experiencing a sort of amnesia when faced with new challenges. Yet, by acknowledging and embracing our past achievements and the lessons learned along the way, we can draw strength and confidence to overcome whatever obstacles lie ahead. Everyone has their own set of facts; it's just a matter of remembering and utilizing them to our advantage.

**Reflection on Leadership Style:**

The TEACH principle has profoundly shaped my leadership style, enhancing my patience, communication clarity, empowerment, engagement, and adaptability. One significant lesson I've learned is to recognize and respect that everyone learns differently, with unique capacities and backgrounds. This realization humbled me and encouraged me to be more intentional about clarity in teaching. I've become more creative in my presentations, striving to illustrate points effectively.

Moreover, I've learned not to take it personally if someone doesn't grasp a concept immediately. Understanding that we all have different perspectives and learning styles has led me to extend patience to both others and myself throughout the learning process.

Furthermore, I've realized the importance of crystal-clear communication. Recognizing past instances where gaps in information led to misunderstandings, I now take ownership of ensuring clarity in my communication. For instance, during a sales refresher workshop, I emphasized the significance of allowing the customer to speak after asking for the sale, with the phrase "First to speak loses" driving home the importance of listening in sales interactions.

During a companywide call audit, I came across a recorded call where a sales agent closed a deal, but then an awkward silence followed. The customer seemed confused and eventually had to prompt the agent with a "helloooo?" Afterward, when questioned about the incident, the agent explained that they remained silent because they remembered my instruction: "First one that speaks after the close loses."

This misunderstanding highlighted a crucial communication gap. I had assumed that my directive was clear, but clearly, it wasn't interpreted as intended. This humbling experience made me realize the importance of being crystal clear in my communication. It taught me that what seems obvious to me may not be so clear to others.

Moving forward, I made a conscious effort to ensure that my instructions and expectations were communicated clearly and effectively, then checked for understanding by asking questions to assess for clarity, leaving no room for misinterpretation. It was a valuable lesson in the importance of clarity and understanding in communication, which I carried with me in all aspects of my leadership journey.

Once I began effectively leveraging the teaching aspect of leadership and ensuring comprehension among my team members, it brought a newfound sense of freedom. I discovered that by equipping them with the necessary knowledge and skills, I could empower and encourage them more effectively. Tasks became clearer, and they embraced the excitement of taking ownership and completing them independently.

With everyone more engaged and proactive, the need for firefighting diminished, allowing us to focus on growth and progress. It was a beautiful transformation to witness as my team took charge and prevented issues before they arose.

As they felt increasingly valued and recognized as emerging leaders, it inspired my own evolution as a communicator. I became more intentional about valuing people in every interaction, both at work and beyond. My goal was for everyone I encountered to feel special, and I passed on this mindset to my team, teaching them to do the same. It was a rewarding journey of growth and empowerment for us all.

**Chapter 5 Key Points to Focus On:**

**Clear and Assumption-Free Communication:**

Assumptions in communication lead to misunderstandings and disengagement. Prioritize clarity and ensure that everyone is on the same page by checking for understanding.

**Empathy in Leadership:**

Empathy is essential for building trust and connection within a team. By understanding and considering the emotions and perspectives of your team members, you can create a supportive and productive work environment.

**Teaching and Developing Others:**

Teaching is a cornerstone of effective leadership. By sharing your knowledge and guiding your team's growth, you not only empower them but also reinforce a culture of continuous learning and improvement.

**Three-Step Action Plan:**

Ensure Clarity in Communication:

Action: Before finalizing any directive or feedback, clearly articulate your expectations and verify understanding.

Implementation: After discussing a task or goal, ask your team member to repeat back their understanding of it. This will help confirm that your message is received as intended.

**Lead with Empathy:**

Action: Approach every interaction with a mindset of empathy, aiming to understand your team members' emotions and perspectives.

Implementation: Practice active listening by acknowledging their feelings and experiences. Use empathetic language, such as, "I can see how this situation might be challenging for you," to create a more supportive atmosphere.

**Commit to Teaching and Mentorship:**

Action: Make teaching and developing your team an ongoing priority.

Implementation: Schedule regular one-on-one sessions with team members to discuss their personal and professional goals. Use these sessions to offer guidance, share relevant experiences, and encourage them to take on new challenges that foster growth.

By focusing on these areas and following the action plans, leaders can effectively enhance communication, start building deeper connections with their teams, and foster a culture of continuous development.

# Chapter 6:
# MODEL

### Leading by Example

John Maxwell once illustrated the contrast between a travel agent and a tour guide to highlight the importance of leadership credibility. He explained that while a travel agent may suggest exotic destinations they've never visited, a tour guide personally leads you to familiar places, sharing intimate details and insider knowledge.

From this analogy, I've learned the critical role of having a body of work, or "facts," to support leadership. Without a proven track record or firsthand experience, leaders struggle to gain trust and buy-in from their teams. Providing guidance without solid facts undermines credibility and breeds suspicion.

As a leader and teacher, it's essential to lead by example and demonstrate expertise in the areas you guide others. Transparency and authenticity build trust, as team members respect leaders who acknowledge their strengths and areas for growth. Admitting when you lack knowledge fosters a culture of continuous learning and improvement.

Some leaders mistakenly believe they must have all the answers, fearing vulnerability. However, true effectiveness comes from humility and a willingness to learn alongside your team. If leaders cannot model the behaviors they expect, they risk losing credibility and effectiveness in their leadership role.

**Modeling Authentic Leadership:**

Decades ago, there was a parental saying that stated, "Do as I say, not as I do." As a kid, this even raised eyebrows and made kids question things, as it discredited that parental figure and cast them into the perception of a joke. These parents who recited that statement would lose credibility. Unfortunately, I've seen so-called leaders with imposter syndrome damage relationships and trust needed to lead a team because they came into leadership with that parent-to-child approach.

People will be able to identify who is real and who is fake easily, especially those who have tenure. There is a gap in today's leadership development that shows the focus shifting from relationship building to more operational, analytical, and administrative development. This helps create imposter syndromes, and you have newfound leaders trying to "fake it until they make it," which truly challenges authentic and trustworthy leadership.

True authentic leadership offers vulnerability and humility, stating that if you do not know how to do something, you should stand in front of that and admit it over faking it. This builds relationships and respect from all. Then, I will be aggressive in learning how to minimize the gaps in things that need to be learned. Development and growth is an ongoing process that should never end for anyone, especially leaders.

## Reflection on Personal Journey:

Robin Burdick called me into her office one late morning and shared some feedback with me: I needed to smile more. She mentioned that several people had mentioned my demeanor wasn't inviting and could come across as intimidating. My initial reaction was to defend myself, emphasizing how laid-back and fun-loving I am. I explained that when I'm focused on work, I may not be smiling because I have my "game face" on.

Robin listened patiently, then leaned back in her chair, removed her glasses, and smiled. With a pause, she asked me to consider something profound: if all those positive attributes I claimed were truly part of me, why weren't people noticing them instead of focusing on my lack of a smile?

Her words hit me hard. It made me realize that the image I thought I was projecting didn't match how others perceived me. This was a pivotal moment in my leadership journey, teaching me the importance of aligning my actions with my true character and intentions. It was a lesson I would carry with me as I continued to grow and develop as a leader.

From that pivotal moment onward, I made a conscious effort to align my actions with my values, understanding that actions speak louder than words. Recognizing that my body language and facial expressions needed improvement, I prioritized speaking, smiling, and engaging with everyone I encountered. This extended to acts of service, whether it was holding doors open, offering a listening ear, or showing flexibility in my schedule to accommodate others.

As I embraced a servant leadership mentality, I moved beyond simply following the "Golden Rule" of treating others as I'd like to be treated. Instead, I aspired to emulate Christ's example of inclusivity, love, grace, mercy, forgiveness, and hope for all. This shift in perspective proved highly effective in my interactions and leadership approach.

Even now, I continue to live out these principles daily, understanding that modeling isn't just about showcasing behaviors—it's about embodying them authentically. To truly inspire others, I must genuinely live out the values I espouse. That's the essence of effective modeling: living what you preach and leading by example.

## Humorous Anecdotes:

In the journey of modeling development, instant success is a myth. It's a process that requires practice, repetition, and learning from mistakes. I vividly recall an incident involving an aspiring leader who was eager to deliver a message to a group of experienced associates. Despite my offer to step in, the leader insisted they were ready to go it alone.

Predictably, the outcome wasn't as smooth as hoped. Feedback from the team confirmed what I had anticipated. However, instead of feeling discouraged, I saw it as a valuable learning experience for the leader. By allowing them to go through it, they gained firsthand insight into the importance of proper preparation and practice.

Reflecting on this experience together, we both chuckled at the lessons learned. The leader then embarked on a journey of observation and practice. They attended various modeling sessions I conducted, and we even created a safe space for practice sessions.

Over time, this leader grew significantly in their modeling skills. They embraced the process, understanding that true mastery comes from consistent practice and dedication. Eventually, they emerged as a confident and effective model, embodying the principles they preached. This journey taught us both the value of respecting the process and the power of persistent effort in personal and professional growth.

**Consistency in Role Modeling:**

Michael Jordan's approach to every game resonated deeply with me. He understood that every performance could leave a lasting impression on someone witnessing him play for the first time. Inspired by this mindset, I adopted a similar approach to modeling.

I recognized that I might not always know when someone was observing my actions, but I was determined to lead authentically and with purpose. Whether it was demonstrating patience, empathy, or simply lending a listening ear, I strived to embody qualities that added value to others' lives.

By consistently modeling these behaviors, I aimed to imprint a positive impact on those around me. It became second nature, much like breathing — effortless and instinctive. Through disciplined practice, I ingrained these values into my daily interactions, making them a fundamental part of who I am as a leader.

Just as Michael Jordan put his best foot forward on the court, I endeavored to do the same in my role. I understood the power of consistency and the profound influence it could have on shaping others' perceptions and experiences. With each interaction, I aimed to leave a lasting impression that reflected my commitment to leadership, development, and adding value to those I encountered.

## Capturing Challenges and Rewards:

Facing challenges served as a test to see if I truly embodied the principles I preached. One of the key lessons I learned was the importance of asking clarifying questions before making assumptions. This practice became a cornerstone of my leadership style, and I made a conscious effort to model it consistently.

By repeatedly demonstrating the value of probing for clarity, I was able to empower other leaders to adopt the same approach. During meetings, I would showcase real-life examples of how failing to ask clarifying questions could lead to misunderstandings and undermine one's leadership credibility.

This experience was eye-opening for many, as they realized the significance of effective communication and the dangers of making assumptions. It became an area of significant growth opportunity for myself and those I mentored. Through this process, I not only reinforced my commitment to practicing what I preached but also helped others develop into more effective leaders by emphasizing the importance of clarity and understanding in all interactions.

## Connection to Second Pillar:

The ability to teach a concept in a way that captivates and stimulates thought is incredibly impactful. When coupled with real-life examples and modeling, the concept truly comes to life. Seeing it in action makes it more tangible and helps solidify the lesson in people's minds.

When a teacher models the behavior or concept they're teaching, it transforms something abstract into something concrete. It sets a clear example for others to follow and provides a tangible goal for personal growth. By witnessing the concept in action, learners can better understand how to apply it in their own lives and strive towards improvement.

## Impact on Team Dynamics:

The modeling approach had a significant positive impact on my team. It gave them a clear roadmap for their development journey, allowing them to envision what progress looked like and get excited about the transformation ahead. Of course, it wasn't always easy. There were challenges along the way, but as they say, growth often comes from discomfort.

This approach also instilled a greater sense of professionalism within the team and fostered the creation of a strong culture we affectionately called "Bad Boy." Despite the unconventional name, it symbolized bringing your best effort and leaving excuses behind. We embraced the idea that success, work-life balance, health, and professionalism could all coexist harmoniously.

Within our "Bad Boy" culture, there was a commitment to excellence and accountability. We held ourselves to high standards, both in performance and appearance. Dressing well and upholding a professional demeanor became ingrained in our identity, shaping the way others perceived us and reinforcing our commitment to success.

In essence, the culture we cultivated was a reflection of our values and collaborative expectations. We understood that we would only achieve what we demanded of ourselves and that tolerating anything less would only hinder our progress. As the saying goes, "You get what you demand, and you encourage what you tolerate." This mindset fueled our growth and drove us toward our goals.

**Chapter 6 Key Points to Focus On:**

**Leading by Example:**

Credibility in leadership comes from a proven track record and the ability to model the behaviors and values you wish to see in your team. Authenticity and transparency are key in building trust.

**Consistency in Actions:**

Consistency in modeling desired behaviors reinforces trust and respect. Whether it's patience, empathy, or professionalism, consistently embodying these traits makes them second nature and sets a standard for others to follow.

**Growth Through Challenges:**

Embracing challenges as opportunities for growth allows both leaders and their teams to develop. By modeling resilience and a commitment to continuous learning, leaders inspire their teams to persevere through difficulties.

**Three-Step Action Plan:**

Model the Behavior You Expect:

Action: Identify key behaviors and values you want to see in your team, such as professionalism, empathy, or dedication.

Implementation: Consistently demonstrate these behaviors in your daily interactions. For example, if you value punctuality, always be on time for meetings and expect the same from your team. Your actions should align with your words, reinforcing the standards you set.

**Be Transparent and Admit Gaps:**

Action: Build trust by being open about your own learning journey and areas where you may lack knowledge or experience.

Implementation: When faced with a challenge outside your expertise, admit it and involve your team in finding solutions. This not only fosters a culture of continuous learning but also shows that it's okay not to have all the answers.

**Encourage and Guide Through Challenges:**

Action: Use challenges as teaching moments for yourself and your team. Show them how to approach obstacles with a growth mindset.

Implementation: When a team member encounters a challenge, guide them through it by sharing your own experiences. Provide support, but also encourage them to take the lead in finding solutions, reinforcing their growth and confidence.

By focusing on these key areas and implementing this action plan, leaders can effectively model the behaviors they wish to see, build stronger relationships with their teams, and foster an environment of continuous improvement.

# Chapter 7:

# COACH

**Leading by Example Coach**

**Nurturing Potential**

In the Bible, one of the most profound examples of Jesus Christ's role as a coach is His interaction with Peter after the resurrection, as recorded in John 21:15-17. What's profound is during the Last Supper, Jesus explained that Peter would deny knowing Him 3 times prior to His crucifixion. With this unfolding, upon Jesus' return, Jesus asks Peter three times if he loves Him, and each time Peter affirms his love, Jesus responds with a command to take care of His followers: "Feed my lambs," "Take care of my sheep," and "Feed my sheep."

This exchange is not merely a conversation but a significant coaching moment where Jesus prepares Peter for his future role as a leader among the disciples. By emphasizing responsibility and leadership, Jesus demonstrates not only the love, compassion, grace, and forgiveness needed to develop those who fall short but also the importance of how critical it is in coaching and developing servant leaders. Modeling, the essential qualities of guidance, encouragement, and accountability in effective leadership.

Coaching is crucial for the success of your team and the overall development of your leaders. Too long has there been ineffective coaching centered around giving orders and directives over teaching, nurturing, and equipping. When an organization can truly master this piece, they will see greater engagement, greater morale, stronger retention, productivity increases, and an environment that people want to be in because they are truly valued.

In this chapter, we will take a deeper look into the impact of coaching and servant leadership on traditional leadership. Coaching is a servant leader's responsibility to produce more leaders. They focus primarily on the growth and well-being of the leaders they are developing and the team to which they belong. Traditional leadership is generally self-centered, focusing on the accumulation and exercise of power and being at the top. When you leverage the momentum around this cultural movement, this is a game changer, and the transformation of your team into highly effective coaches is only eminent.

**Coaching as a Pillar:**

Coaching is very crucial as it can make or break teams, and organizations should prioritize the bulk of their leadership development in this area of developing great coaches. Effective coaches have the power to maximize everyone's full, true potential.

When this happens, everyone wins, and a winning culture becomes established that can turn into a dominant, very productive one.

On the other hand, if organizations go into this area of development half-heartedly, then you risk having an environment that may lack a strong work ethic and trust and, unfortunately, develop a tolerance for negotiable standards and poor results. Associates who see the lack of leadership investment in their immediate coaches may disregard truly taking ownership of their own results, thus producing results that waiver from one point of the spectrum to the other. Furthermore, this inadvertently sends internal messaging that may show that the organization doesn't really stand behind the product or service it provides, thus creating in-house net detractors. Therefore, accountability is scarce, and the excuses are rampant because they're doing what they are being led to do by their underdeveloped coaches.

**Servant Leadership:**

Unfortunately, I've heard many people state they were servant leaders, but their actions contradicted that claimed identity.

The concept of servant leadership was formally introduced by Robert K. Greenleaf in his 1970 essay, "The Servant as Leader." Greenleaf, an American management expert, was inspired by his experience in corporate America and his reading of Hermann Hesse's short novel "Journey to the East." In his essay, Greenleaf articulated the idea that the most effective leaders prioritize serving others, including employees, customers, and the community, rather than seeking power or control for themselves.

Servant leadership, as described by Greenleaf, focuses on the growth and well-being of people and the communities to which they belong. A servant leader shares power, puts the needs of others first, and helps people develop and perform to the best of their abilities. This philosophy contrasts with traditional leadership models that emphasize hierarchical authority and the accumulation of power by leaders.

While Greenleaf formalized the concept in modern organizational theory, the true principles of servant leadership can be traced back to Jesus Christ, who exemplified serving others as a fundamental aspect of leadership, accomplishing this with the following attributes:

- *Love*
- *Patience*
- *Gentleness*
- *Peace*
- *Patience*
- *Kindness*
- *Long-suffering*
- *Forgiving*

- *Humility*
- *Self-Control*
- *Fairness*
- *Dependable*

This list is humbling and is an attribute I deemed a priority to learn, embody, develop, and exhibit. These are the TMC foundational principles that have become more apparent and applicable in the coaching realm. The main focal point of effective coaching is the relationship established between the coach and the coach. The energy should be on valuing that person being coached, making them feel safe, empowered, equipped, and excited for growth and execution gains. This is what a servant-leader focuses primarily on the growth and well-being of people and the communities to which they belong.

While traditional leadership generally involves the accumulation and exercise of power by one at the "top of the pyramid," often devaluing people in the process. Whereas ... The servant-leader not only shares power but empowers and puts the needs of others first. While helping people develop and perform as highly as possible, providing hope ... helping other people excel.

When you build relationships from the foundational Christ attributes identified, you get relationships that foster trust, respect, and admiration for that leader providing the development. When associates are in their presence, they openly lean in over being distant and on guard, ready to defend themselves from ridicule and/or a devaluing conversation.

**Practical Tips:**

First and foremost, establishing a transparent and authentic relationship with your team members is a high priority. Sure, it's important to know about their birthdays, anniversaries, family members, things that are of interest to them, hobbies, etc., as well as that same knowledge of yourself being extended and offered to them. All of that is helpful, no doubt. It's also imperative that you understand their learning and communication styles and preferences.

One of the biggest things to know is their "why." This is huge. Knowing the origins of where their why comes from, why it's important to them, and how they envision acquiring whatever is needed to obtain their why. Knowing this equips leaders with the ability not only to use motivation but also, more importantly, leverage inspiration in their own way.

When you know all these things, the next step is to be able to act on this information immediately, slowly, steadily, and without fail because now they want to see how you apply this treasure chest of information as well. Now is the time to prove your authenticity towards them because, most likely, they have been bamboozled by leadership members who say one thing and then do something completely different, sending "mixed signals."

Leverage technology now. I would recommend using your cell phone and now start placing contact information of your team members, highlighting birthdays, anniversaries, and any special notes needed about them – their why. Then, create reminders of important events they shared with you, and now act on these things.

Sending text messages for their birthdays or special dates. Being proactive with scheduling needs and discussing ahead of time anniversaries that will be coming up, holiday plans for their family, special outings, new video game releases, etc., whatever is important to them. Even random calls on their days off to thank them for showing up every day or recognizing something that normally gets taken for granted, and now showing value to them. Usually, when an associate gets a phone call on their off time, it's normally not followed with praise but with something they did wrong or didn't do or the need to come to work some overtime.

Leveraging this TMC methodology, you now must be the advocate for building this relationship to truly show that you do care and that you want to foster and establish a nurturing, real, authentic relationship with them.

I remember conducting several experiments (focused on the modeling aspect of TMC) with my leadership team. We were going through a season in which we had an unprecedentedly higher call volume than expected, and we needed to solicit overtime. My team expressed how frustrating it was that several of their own team members were not answering their phones when they were calling to ask people to come in and work. The phrase they kept using was how their own team members were "ghosting" them. I laughed as I thought about some of the opportunities that were apparent to establish relationships.

On a random Saturday, I identified which leadership team members were off, and I proceeded to call them. Over half of them answered the first time I called. I explained immediately that I'd be quick and that I was not recruiting for overtime (so that they didn't become anxious), and I showered them with adoration at how they'd been handling themselves during this season of high volume. Then I begged them to have a great rest of their off time and hung up. The others that didn't answer initially called me back, explaining that they saw I called. I said the same things to them and proceeded to hang up without fielding a response. The shock factor was real! The appreciation was real. The approach was something none of them had ever experienced or witnessed. This was a game-changer.

The following week, each of these team members came into my office expressing shock and appreciation for that experience. They felt valued and knew that it was genuine. Some even expressed the shock of hanging up at the end, which really caught them off guard, but they smiled immediately after that call.

So, as I sat on that experiment, two things entered my mind. First, my opportunity to do this more often was sobering. Secondly, I identified none of them were able to connect the dots as to what I did to them and the current environment that exists in their units. Both realizations were critical for us to evolve. Building stronger relationships opens the door to creating more stakeholders for your team.

During one of our weekly leadership huddles, I brought out what I did and asked those involved to share their experience with the many who weren't involved. They all shared similar emotions, and some even thought I was going to call back and now ask for them to come help, but that never happened. They were all super appreciative of that act.

I then asked how many had ever done anything like that for their team, and I heard the crickets in the next county over any voice assembled there. I took ownership and stated that I should be doing more of that period. Then, I encouraged them to follow suit and immediately start looking for ways to call their team members and just show them some love and appreciation for what they do.

Some leaders not involved stated one reason my calls were answered was most likely because of my position. I validated that observation and agreed that it could've been factual. Then I asked everyone to envision a world in which, regardless of anyone's position, people felt compelled to answer the call because of who was calling and the experience they had with that person. I stated that's the type of relationship we all should be striving for. "Light Bulbs" came on, and they got it, as this was all brought on by the Teach, Model, and Coach premise. This was a teaching moment from the modeling I provided and the ownership of my responsibility of developing and modeling next-level leadership. It was real, authentic, and transparent.

**Engaging Stories:**

I have been referenced as the analogy king due to how I teach using this concept, especially using sports as a focal point to drive execution. Yet, it was evident to me that I used sports too much and needed to customize my approach due to my audience or the person I was engaged with; now, that's truly valuing people on another level.

Furthermore, I identified the power of placing someone in my shoes "theoretically" so that they can see the challenges that I am seeing at that moment. Once I started to develop this, it became a powerful tool to use as I grew in how to effectively use it. One classic moment I utilized this approach was with a bunch of tenured associates who were not performing well. They were inconsistent in hitting their numbers and had more excuses as to why their results were poor. They had no accountability, and this was becoming frustrating on my end. I needed them to see this from my perspective without devaluing any of them.

When I took stock of who was involved, I realized that the majority experienced some failed relationships and that they were all parents trying to keep their households afloat. The majority were leading a single-parent household.

I gave them a scenario and asked them to imagine if they were in the situation I was presenting and how they would handle it. The scenario I created was that they were in a relationship with their child's mother/father, and one day, the partner came home visibly upset because, without warning, cutbacks took place, and they were let go. I asked what they would do at that moment. Unanimously, they all stated they would comfort, console, and provide encouragement and support.

Then I explained that for the next several weeks, their mate was actively looking for employment but was coming up empty. Yet, they were picking up the kids from school or daycare, cleaning their place, having dinner ready, and taking the lead on all the domestic affairs to show that they were doing their part. I asked what they would do then. Once again, unanimously, they all stated they would acknowledge their efforts and just encourage them, telling their mate that something is bound to become available for them.

Now, I took it on a different path. I explained that after two and half months of no success, they started to see their mate become a little defeated. This was evident because they were not as active as before in pursuing leads, and all the domestic components started to lack attention; dishes were now in the sink, dinner was occasionally ready, and the cleanliness of their dwelling was lacking as well. I asked, what would they do? Now, I started to see mixed views.

Only a couple stated that he or she had to go! I was shocked and reminded them that this was their baby daddy or mommy, and that did not change their decision. Again, that was only 2-3 of the 8 gathered. The others chimed in and said they would help coach the partner on interviewing and selling themselves better. They also stated that they would even sit down and look at job openings to help identify any opportunities being overlooked or dismissed. I then asked how long they would allow this to go on from this point, and they all responded that it depended on how well their partner took the feedback/coaching.

At this point, I had everyone where I wanted. Now, I presented the following scenario. It's now over 4 months gone by. No longer is their mate doing anything in their dwelling. The place is not clean. Dishes are in the sink. Kids are not being picked up or cared for, the electric and water bills are skyrocketing out of control, video games are the focus point all day for their partner, and all the responsibilities fall on them. Before I asked what any of them would do, they all said … "that person has to go!" I laughed and reminded them that this was their baby daddy/mommy, and unanimously, they all said, "I don't care who they are. I'm not playing that game!" I laughed and laughed and stated you all are heartless.

They explained that prior to the hard times, there was a mutual agreement that they would be a team and not one person would carry all the burden of their success as a family. Many of them stated that after they kicked their partner out, if they in the future got their act together, defined as finding a job and maturing into a more responsible person, they may consider inviting them back. Yet, at that time frame, they said they could do bad by themselves, and their partner still must go. No ifs, ands, or buts about it. I told them that they were all hardcore and that if they were ever bosses, I would not want to work for them.

Then, in a very dramatic fashion, I brought out all their results for the last 5 months (November through March). I laid each of their status reports directly in front of them. I pointed out that there are 5 months of results that are not meeting the agreed-upon expectation for their results. I also made it clear that unlike their personal decisions to ultimately fire their significant others after just over 3 months or poor performance, this is not the case for them and that they still have "keys to the house" and a place to call home, but now, for how long with these current results?

I then clearly stated that if it were their decision, they all would be fired now based on that little scenario I brought them through.

Their response was "Silence."

I then responded that I'm not trying to fire anyone. I stated that some things in this household must change and that I cannot burden myself with this. They got it! This team went from being second to last on the floor to the number one team that year (out of 23 total teams, and did this in a span of 9 months). They all changed their mindsets and took and applied the feedback and coaching provided.

There was another situation in which I had a leadership team member who played baseball and was on a level that almost made it into the majors. He was an athlete and knew baseball as this was his life.

He approached me in my office and wanted to take some harsh disciplinary action towards a team member he had for failure to follow a process or procedure. In the initial meeting we had, I asked if this was something he "felt" strongly about, taking severe action like that. His response was yes. I backed him and said okay.

I asked him to gather all the facts about this situation. This is defined as talking with this team member first and identifying their knowledge of this procedure being missed or not executed as expected. I also wanted to see all the coaching documentation showing that this team member was equipped and that they could execute without fail. I also wanted to see how many occurrences this team member failed to execute and all the teaching, modeling, and coaching that took place in those situations as well.

My leadership team member said no problem and went to start gathering all the requested information. Shortly afterward, he returned with a look of amazement on his face. Explaining that his team member had no clue that he was doing this procedure incorrectly and was utilizing guidance he received some time ago from another leader. Now, he realizes that procedures have changed and that he assumed this team member knew.

At that moment, I brought it back to baseball. I gave a scenario that would involve him back in his playing baseball days. Knowing that he played for different teams and coaches, I set the situation up in which he started playing for a new team. I asked that while he learned some simple basic signs to bunt or steal, would it be fair to assume the new team he went to play for used the same signs? He laughed and said of course not.

I then sat there and asked how he would feel if his new coaches just assumed that he would know the new signs because everyone on the team knows them, but somehow, he missed this. But because you're not comprehending signs that are being given, you seem to disregard direction, and now they want to cut you. He said, "T, it actually wouldn't go down like that, but I get it." I asked why it was, and he wouldn't state that he would not let it go there because he pays attention to detail, and that would never happen.

I then asked if we were simply playing an assumption game and if it isn't dangerous to allow our implicit biases to creep into our leadership path, causing us to have distractions of, this person should have known this or that, and/or I would never do this or that because I'm detailed oriented so, everyone should be just as detailed oriented if they really cared.

This leadership team member sat there and just looked at me with his mouth open and eyes wide open, and now he was able to see. Nearly tearing up realizing that our decisions and actions impact real people. Yes, human beings want to do good, and it's our responsibility to truly be servant leaders. After this leader recognized the opportunity, he changed his approach, showing value to his team members, and taught, modeled, and coached to remove the deficient execution that was previously taking place around a procedure.

**Unlocking Full Potential:**

As with all growth aspects, every team member progressed based on that individual's growth potential and the work they put into developing their skill. Yet, within all of them, I was able to see the confidence building in each as they progressed. I used to have them practice by recording themselves having certain coaching conversations while using a framework/outline. They made this more of a competition against their peers like an "American Idol," and this pushed all of them and the quality of work that would represent them. Now, we have started to talk about their body of work or their brand and what that would look like. This entire method heightened their holistic approach to serving those they were coaching, and the momentum gained from this was powerful.

This transferred over to their written communication and how their emails were also their brand that speaks to their body of work. Specifically, I learned how the content was organized, the message it was conveying, the objective and the clarity of the communication, and what the next steps would be afterward as a result. The coaching development helped with their emails, making them clearer and listing action items as to how something was going to happen. The overall ownership of their body of work grew immensely because of their coaching development.

One of the foundational thought processes I placed into their mindsets is that growing into an effective coach was an ongoing process and journey until they took their last breath. Often, I have seen too many fool themselves by thinking they've arrived, thus plateauing their own growth and then leveling out within that realm of theirs. I used to call this "fake news." I shaped it in the sense that if you're interacting with people, you must be ever-evolving and growing. People change, and changing is constant and always in motion, and so must an effective leader be in their ability to serve people with their coaching execution.

Because of the way I had a hands-on approach, often assessing real-time coaching exhibitions from my team, I had a strong grasp of assessing who was maturing in their effectiveness. Once this was identified, I would then start putting these leaders into scenarios and positions, and they would now lead weekly results meetings with the entire team. This provided them a platform to see how they performed with peer-to-peer communication, coaching, and leading. In this environment, it was clear to see who exactly was closer to next-level leadership, which organizationally would be from supervisor to manager, then director, and then assistant vice president.

I was fortunate to have equipped, developed, and promoted over 30+ associates from sales entry-level positions into the leadership branches. Ranging from coaches all the way up to directors. This cemented my own ability in my body of work to develop effective leaders and make them all effective coaches as well.

**Building a High-Performing Workforce:**

When people are equipped, and they know, without a shadow of a doubt, what to do and how to do it, and know that they have someone there to truly coach them, it's powerful. Because now you get to marry their potential talent and equipping to a narrative that they create.

*What do I mean by this?*

Knowing their "why" provides fuel for their execution and success. Having them tune into the radio station "WII-FM" (What's In It For Me) now puts them into the seat of being a stakeholder, and the concern of their own body of work rises because they know the yield and the impact on their whys. Motivation is good for short-term goals, and it helps create momentum.

When one develops as an effective coach, one is able to leverage the equipping, teaching, and valuing of potential talent and associates to create a high-performance work environment where people feel valued. The communication is uplifting. The goals are clear. The equipping is constant, and associates are always stretched to execute on their top-tier levels, showing consistency. Results are shared and offer a natural environment of competitiveness.

Adding contests, incentives, and recognition that show appreciation for all people performing creates a successful work environment. Also, providing help, support, and nurturing to those who have not yet reached their potential provides hope, not fear, in an environment filled with valuing people. Lastly, differentiating the value of appreciation shown to those who perform above average truly provides a successful blueprint for a high-performing, motivated, and inspired workforce. This is all accomplished with effective coaching.

What I experienced was a transformation of individual teams performing into an overall community awakening. This means that our entire sales team started to take great pride in the overall body of work that was being produced from a holistic approach in which everyone was a potential stakeholder in our overall success. Then, when the actual stats were communicated across the floor, our team wanted to lead the company in all aspects of selling. This was a beautiful surprise I was not expecting, yet it was a testament to the culture that was being developed: "You get what you demand, you encourage what you tolerate." Again, with a high priority on the inputs and the coaching effectiveness, the outputs confirmed the work going into it.

If you're able to marry the talent to the know-how, people tend to gain confidence. Then, when you're able to show the facts associated with that, you start to build a team that becomes a force with which to be reckoned.

**Connection to previous Pillars:**

When people feel respected, valued, and safe, they will perform. Building off of the foundations of your teaching approach helps support the buy-in from your team members. The value-added approach of explaining whatever the objective is, the why, the anticipated output, the implementation date, and how this will look with detailed training and equipping outline sets a strong foundation. Followed up with modeling that validates the consistency in the vision and the valuing of people are the building blocks for this stage of TMC.

Without these things already in place, then the dynamic between traditional leadership and servant leadership will increasingly be exposed in an atmosphere where people may feel like all they get are "marching orders" and are expected to march flawlessly. Not a good look at all.

So it's paramount that from the beginning, your leadership or leadership team embraces the pillars introduced earlier, actively grows within those attributes, and effectively puts them all into play. This will allow for the continued overlaying of stronger servant leadership attributes that yield an overwhelming engagement and buy-in from the team.

**Impact on Motivation:**

The impact on motivation for the leadership was a newfound awareness of what was possible. Team members were motivated to learn this approach so that they could be equipped to do the same within their teams, their households, and their relationships, and they wanted to replicate this approach asap. Furthermore, it opened their eyes to start identifying more of their "why," meaning their inspirations, and seeing the difference between the two.

Motivations identified as short-term goals they were going for, which helped fuel their tanks. Inspirations, though, are now being identified as long-term, more personal focuses on creating legacies or safety for their families, their non-negotiables, standards, and values one never relinquishes, in which these identified focuses truly help in pursuit of their dreams. This helped get them all fired up! The total result was that everyone started to increase the level of coaching, both on a frequency and effectiveness level. This was great to see.

**Chapter 7 Key Points to Focus On:**

**Coaching as a Pillar of Leadership:**

Effective coaching is crucial for unlocking the full potential of team members. It involves nurturing, teaching, and developing others to create a culture of growth, accountability, and high performance.

**Servant Leadership Attributes:**

Servant leadership, rooted in attributes like love, patience, humility, and self-control, emphasizes the growth and well-being of others. This leadership style fosters trust, respect, and a positive work environment.

**Building Relationships and Trust:**

Establishing authentic and transparent relationships with team members is essential. Understanding their motivations, communication styles, and personal interests creates a foundation of trust and mutual respect.

**Three-Step Action Plan:**

**Develop and Practice Servant Leadership:**

Action: Prioritize the well-being and growth of your team members by embodying servant leadership attributes such as patience, humility, and empathy.

Implementation: Regularly engage with your team to understand their needs and aspirations. Offer support, guidance, and encouragement in a way that aligns with their personal and professional goals.

**Create Authentic Connections:**

Action: Build genuine relationships with your team by getting to know their motivations and inspirations, personal interests, and communication preferences.

Implementation: Leverage technology to keep track of important dates and details about your team members. Actively show appreciation and recognition through personalized messages or calls, especially during special occasions.

**Model Consistency and Accountability:**

Action: Consistently model the behaviors and values you expect from your team. Be transparent and accountable in your actions.

Implementation: Lead by example in your daily interactions. When addressing performance issues, use real-life scenarios to help your team understand the impact of their actions and the importance of accountability. Encourage open communication and provide ongoing feedback to support their growth.

By implementing these steps, leaders can foster a culture of growth, trust, and high performance, leading their teams with authenticity and purpose.

# Chapter 8:
# The Domino Effect

When I think about the domino effect, I see it as a powerful metaphor for how one small action can set off a chain of events that grows larger and more impactful as it moves forward. Just like a line of dominoes falling one after another when the first one is tipped over, the domino effect represents how a single event can trigger a series of related events.

This concept isn't just limited to one area of life; it shows up everywhere. Whether it's in economics, politics, social changes, or even natural phenomena, a small trigger can lead to a much bigger reaction. This ripple effect can transform entire situations, environments, or even cultures over time.

Let me share an example from my own experience with teaching, modeling, and coaching. I've noticed how the ripple effect plays out in the context of identity change and its impact on an environment, particularly in the culture of a sales unit. By consistently teaching and coaching others, I've seen how small changes in behavior or mindset can lead to significant transformations. It starts with one person making a shift, perhaps embracing a new way of thinking or adopting a new strategy. That change influences others around them, creating a ripple effect that spreads through the team or organization.

I had an incredible experience that really highlighted the power of leadership and the impact we can have on others. On my YouTube channel, I created a series called "Leadership Reflections," where I shared over 20 videos capturing my journey as a leader. Growing up in the corporate world, especially at GEICO, I went through a significant transformation, learning and growing from the leaders who guided me. As I developed, I made it a point to pass on what I had learned to the leaders I was mentoring, helping them grow in their own journeys.

As the series progressed, something truly special happened in videos 22 and 23. These videos captured my retirement celebration, which was a powerful moment that really showcased the domino effect of teaching, modeling, and coaching. What made it so remarkable was that people from all different backgrounds, some of whom I had never even worked with directly in sales, came forward to share their experiences and the impact I had on them.

Hearing their stories and realizing how my own transformation had influenced them was incredibly moving. It was a clear reminder that the way we lead and the example we set can create ripples far beyond what we might imagine. The celebration wasn't just about my retirement; it was about the lasting impact that teaching, modeling, and coaching had on those around me.

This experience reinforced for me how important it is to be intentional in our actions as leaders. By investing in others and sharing our knowledge and experiences, we can spark a chain reaction that helps others grow and succeed. It's a powerful reminder that the legacy we leave behind isn't just about what we achieve personally but about how we lift others up along the way.

I felt it was crucial to dedicate an entire chapter to exploring the broader impact of the Teach, Model, and Coach (TMC) approach. This chapter delves deeply into what makes TMC so powerful and why it's essential for effective leadership. The TMC approach isn't just another leadership strategy; it's a framework built on three key pillars: teaching, modeling, and coaching. These elements are what set TMC apart and make it so effective in guiding others.

When I compare TMC to other leadership methodologies, it stands out because it embodies true servant leadership, which is fundamentally different from traditional leadership styles. Traditional leadership often focuses on accumulating and exercising power, with leaders prioritizing organizational or personal goals above all else. Their primary concern is often achieving specific outcomes, and the people they lead can sometimes become secondary to these goals.

In contrast, the TMC approach is all about true servant leadership, the kind modeled by Jesus Christ Himself. It emphasizes service, putting the needs of others first, and guiding them with wisdom and compassion. TMC leaders are not just focused on achieving goals; they are committed to helping others grow, learn, and succeed. This kind of leadership is transformative because it nurtures an environment where people feel valued, supported, and inspired to reach their full potential.

By focusing on teaching, modeling, and coaching, TMC leaders create a ripple effect that can have a profound impact on those they lead. They don't just direct; they teach others how to think and act in ways that align with the core values of service and integrity. They don't just set examples; they model the behaviors and attitudes that reflect true leadership. And they don't just oversee; they coach others, providing guidance and encouragement to help them develop their own skills and strengths.

In this chapter, I wanted to highlight how TMC isn't just a leadership style—it's a way of life that brings out the best in everyone involved. It's about leading with purpose, with a focus on service, and creating lasting positive change in the lives of others.

Servant leadership, as modeled by Christ, is all about putting others first. It's not about focusing on yourself but on serving those around you. Jesus taught and lived out this kind of leadership, showing that true leadership is about service, putting the needs of others ahead of your own, and caring for the overall well-being of those you lead.

For me, the moment I truly understood this was a game-changer. It wasn't about "me, me, me" anymore. I began to see leadership from a whole new perspective—one that was less about my own ambitions and more about the team I was leading. I realized that my role wasn't just to manage tasks or achieve sales targets; it was to genuinely care for the people who were coming to me, often with issues that had nothing to do with work. They were sharing real-life situations—problems with family, challenges with friends, and things happening outside of the office that weighed heavily on them.

As I started to listen more intently, to really see and hear the people around me, something powerful happened. They noticed my transformation. They saw the change in my character and my spirit, and, most importantly, they began to trust me. And that trust was huge.

When people trust you, it opens up a whole new level of connection and influence. They feel safe coming to you, not just as a leader but as someone who genuinely cares about their well-being. This shift in focus—from self to others—made me a better leader and created an environment where people felt supported, understood, and valued. That's the essence of servant leadership: it's about serving with an open heart, leading with empathy, and building trust through genuine care and concern for those you lead.

For me, serving others has always been a true blessing. When I fully embraced the Teach, Model, and Coach (TMC) approach, it became a powerful platform for living out this calling. TMC allowed me to deeply root my actions in genuine inspiration, enabling me to serve others in a way that felt both meaningful and impactful.

### Power in Traditional Leadership vs. Servant Leadership

When you compare traditional leadership with servant leadership, the differences are striking. In traditional leadership, power is often used to command and control people. Leaders make decisions based on their authority and the hierarchy within the organization. Their focus is on maintaining control and asserting their position at the top.

But when I look at how Christ modeled servant leadership, it's clear that His use of power was entirely different. His authority wasn't about control—it was about empowerment. Christ used His power to teach, uplift, and encourage others to grow in their capabilities and spiritual understanding. He didn't focus on maintaining control over people; instead, He focused on helping them become the best version of themselves. That's the essence of servant leadership: using your influence to build others up, not to keep them down.

**The Relational Aspect:**

**Keeping Distance vs. Building Connection**

Another significant difference between traditional leadership and servant leadership lies in the relationships leaders build with their team members. Traditional leaders often maintain a distant, authoritative stance. They emphasize their role at the top of the hierarchy, creating a gap between themselves and those they lead. I like to compare this to the Heisman Trophy pose in football: one hand holds the ball close, representing power and authority, while the other hand is extended out, keeping people at a distance.

In contrast, servant leadership is all about closing that distance. It's about building genuine connections with others, breaking down barriers, and fostering a sense of trust and collaboration. Servant leaders don't push people away; they bring them closer, understanding that real strength comes from empowering and connecting with those you lead.

By embracing the principles of TMC and servant leadership, I've found that the impact I can have is so much greater. It's not just about holding onto power—it's about using that power to serve, uplift, and truly connect with others. And in doing so, the blessing of serving becomes even more profound.

## Building Genuine Relationships

With servant leadership, the focus shifts to building real, meaningful relationships with your team members. It's about getting to know people on a personal level, understanding their needs, and expressing genuine care and concern for their lives. Unlike traditional leadership, which can sometimes feel distant and impersonal, servant leadership is all about connecting with people in a way that shows you truly value them as individuals.

Then, there's the modeling aspect of leadership. Traditional leaders might dictate what needs to be done, but true servant leaders, through the Teach, Model, and Coach (TMC) approach, lead by example. They don't just tell you how to live and lead—they show you. A powerful example of this is when Christ washed the feet of His disciples. This was a task usually performed by servants, but Jesus did it to demonstrate humility and the importance of serving others. By modeling this behavior, He taught a valuable lesson: leadership isn't about being above others; it's about being willing to serve them.

## Inspiring Through Intrinsic Motivation

The motivation aspect is another key difference between traditional and servant leadership. Traditional leadership often relies on external motivators, like rewards or punishments. These tactics might work in the short term, but they're often fleeting and don't create lasting change. On the other hand, Jesus' leadership style was characterized by inspiring intrinsic motivation. He didn't just focus on short-term rewards or consequences; He aimed to transform the hearts and minds of people. He guided them towards a love-based approach to others, setting standards and values that were non-negotiable and showing them how to achieve these ideals.

This approach is incredibly powerful because it goes beyond mere rule-following or chasing temporary goals. Instead, it encourages a deep, internal shift that aligns people's actions with their core values, and what inspires them. Servant leadership, as modeled by Christ, isn't about controlling people or pushing them toward quick fixes. It's about inspiring them to reach their full potential by focusing on what truly matters—love, service, and integrity.

## Shifting Focus to Long-Term Impact

When I think about long-term goals, traditional leadership often focuses on specific performance outcomes. These might include hitting certain targets, driving organizational growth, or achieving other success metrics that are usually tied to measurable results. While these goals are important, they often miss a deeper, more meaningful aspect of leadership.

True servant leadership, as exemplified by Christ, is oriented toward something far greater: the spiritual growth and moral development of individuals. It's about nurturing your team, your household, and your community based on values like compassion, justice, and love. For me, this was a truly inspiring realization, especially after losing my dad and reflecting on how society often operates. The relational aspect of servant leadership became a game-changer in my life.

## Leaving a Legacy Through TMC

This shift in perspective drove me to leave a lasting legacy within my organization, my community, and my team. Every day, I felt inspired to get out of bed because I knew I had the opportunity to make a positive impact on someone's life. The Teach, Model, and Coach (TMC) approach became the vehicle for this impact. Through TMC, I could see the ripple effect—the domino effect—of my actions, and it was both humbling and fulfilling.

One particular example that stands out in my mind highlights how TMC fostered collaboration and success. By focusing on serving others, I saw how the values of compassion and justice could bring people together, creating an environment where everyone could thrive. This wasn't just about hitting targets or achieving short-term goals; it was about cultivating a culture where people felt valued, understood, and supported.

I had one supervisor, a very tenured supervisor. They've been with the company for over 20 something years and was still getting settled in Florida as they moved from another state across the country.

I vividly remember a situation with the tenured supervisor where the results and team interactions raised some red flags. It became clear that something needed to change to help this supervisor grow and better support their team. So, we made a bold decision: we temporarily removed the supervisor from their team, almost like taking someone out of their usual environment to go through rehabilitation or physical therapy after an injury.

This process was all about reconditioning and pivoting—giving the supervisor the time and space to develop the skills they needed to succeed. In their place, we introduced an up-and-coming coach to lead the team. Here's the eye-opening part: I personally developed this coach through the Teach, Model, and Coach (TMC) approach. I had been guiding them, not by explicitly labeling it as TMC, but by simply living out these principles in real-time, without making a big announcement about it.

As soon as this coach stepped in, the impact was immediate and profound. The way they applied the TMC methodology created a shift in the team's dynamics. Relationships began to flourish, trust was built, and the team started to operate on a whole new level. It was incredible to witness how this approach, quietly and steadily implemented, could lead to such a positive transformation.

The experience of seeing the transformation in a team simply by changing the leader was nothing short of remarkable. It was the same team with the same members, but when a different coach stepped in, the difference was like night and day. I had been developing this less tenured coach, and as they began to guide the team, the results were astonishing.

During our results meetings, this new leader would present the team's achievements, and I couldn't help but jokingly suggest that maybe they should stay with that team permanently. Looking back, I realize that it might not have been the most tactful way to express value, especially with the more tenured supervisor still in the room. But that more experienced supervisor knew I had nothing but love and respect for them. My actions spoke louder than words—I was dedicated to getting them re-engaged, re-equipped, and ready to return to the floor with renewed vigor.

What really struck me was how quickly the change happened. Within just a month, the team's results began to climb dramatically. It was mind-boggling to witness.

The impact of that experience was truly powerful. The transformation in the team wasn't just about changing the leader; it was about how the new coach's natural strengths and the Teach, Model, and Coach (TMC) methodology came together to create something extraordinary.

This coach had a natural talent for engaging with people and building strong relationships. When these inherent skills were combined with the TMC approach, it was a game-changer for the team. The results were remarkable. The team quickly rose to become a top-quartile performer, showcasing just how effective this blend of personal attributes and leadership principles could be.

This success also opened up new opportunities for the coach. Their exceptional performance earned them a promotion, and when they were given their own team, they led them to become the number one team on the floor. Watching this unfold was incredibly fulfilling. It wasn't just about seeing numbers improve; it was about witnessing how effective leadership and genuine connection can drive exceptional results and career growth.

## Chapter 8 Key Points to Focus On:

*The Domino Effect in Leadership:*

Small, intentional actions in leadership, such as teaching, modeling, and coaching, can create a ripple effect that influences others in profound ways. Leaders must be aware of how their actions impact the larger culture and environment of their team.

*The Power of Servant Leadership:*

Servant leadership focuses on empowering others by prioritizing their needs and growth over personal power. This approach creates deeper connections, fosters trust, and encourages team members to reach their full potential.

*Transformative Impact of TMC (Teach, Model, Coach):*

The TMC approach creates lasting change by focusing on growth, relationships, and development. When leaders effectively teach, model the behaviors they expect, and coach their team, they inspire transformation that leads to both personal and professional success.

*Three-Step Action Plan:*

Initiate the Domino Effect with Small, Intentional Actions:

Action: Start by making small, consistent actions that align with your core values and leadership goals. Focus on teaching, modeling, and coaching in daily interactions.

Implementation: Choose one action each day, whether it's providing constructive feedback, modeling positive behaviors, or coaching a team member on an improvement area. Track the impact over time and adjust your approach as necessary.

*Lead with a Servant's Heart:*

Action: Shift your focus from personal achievements to serving your team's needs and growth. Empower them by listening, guiding, and providing the tools they need to succeed.

Implementation: Spend time getting to know your team members' personal goals, motivations, inspirations, and challenges. Make a commitment to serve their needs by offering support, resources, or mentoring that aligns with their aspirations.

*Transform Your Team with TMC Principles:*

Action: Integrate the Teach, Model, and Coach methodology into your leadership style to create a culture of growth and accountability.

Implementation: Create structured opportunities for teaching moments, model the behavior you expect from your team, and provide regular coaching to guide their development. Celebrate small wins and encourage continuous improvement.

By focusing on these areas, leaders can initiate positive change, empower their teams through servant leadership, and create a lasting impact through the transformative TMC approach.

# Chapter 9:
# Applying Principles At Home

One of the most rewarding aspects of becoming an empty nester is the opportunity to focus entirely on your relationship with your spouse, free from the distractions that kids can bring. This phase offers a unique chance to rediscover the pure, one-on-one connection that forms the foundation of your marriage. Without the interruptions of parenting, you can truly see the potential for growth and deepening within your relationship.

This is where the principles of teaching, modeling, and coaching (TMC) can really shine. While TMC is often applied in the workplace, its beauty lies in how it transcends that environment. These principles are just as effective in personal relationships—whether with your spouse, children, family, or friends. At the core, everyone desires to feel valued and understood.

In my own marriage, I've learned, and continue to learn the importance of recognizing my wife's communication style. Instead of trying to mold it to fit my own, I've embraced a more nurturing and supportive approach. By valuing her way of expressing herself and listening intently to both her words and the emotions behind them, our connection has grown stronger. This mindful approach to communication not only enhances our relationship but also fosters a deeper sense of respect and understanding.

When communicating with your spouse, it's crucial to not just hear their words but to truly understand what they're conveying. Ask yourself questions like, "What's behind this emotion? What triggered it? Where is this coming from?" By digging deeper, you can connect on a more meaningful level and address the underlying concerns.

Now, I know it sounds simple when I explain it, but in that moment, it's often a challenging opportunity for growth. Unlike interactions with coworkers or those you lead, the emotional investment with your spouse is much deeper and more intimate. This is where the real work begins, and for me, it's where I lean on my faith in Jesus Christ.

In those moments, I find comfort in turning to prayer, knowing that I can seek divine guidance at any time. At home, these principles, which are rooted in Christ, take on an even more profound meaning. Without any reservations, I can experience the spiritual depth of my relationship, leaning into faith to navigate the complexities of intimacy and connection.

Even at work, I often found myself thinking, "What would Christ do in this situation?" But at home, that question becomes even more significant. Unlike the workplace, where HR rules and procedures guide interactions, home life is governed solely by God's way and staying in alignment with His will. As the leader of my household, I strive to nurture, support, and love my wife, kids, and friends in a way that leaves them with the essence of Christ—an aroma of grace, love, and life.

But I'm not perfect. If I got it right every time, I'd be "Jesus Junior," as my pastor likes to say. The truth is, I'm still a human being, growing in this aspect of life. Yet, within my conscious being, I'm committed to this journey of growth, aiming to communicate in a way that reflects Christ's love, even if I don't always get it right.

It's now on my cognitive radar—within the 2 to 4% of my consciousness that I actively use with purpose and intention. This awareness is focused on ensuring that my communication is greater, healthier, and more supportive. When I sense, through the body language of whoever I'm speaking with—whether it's my wife, mom, kids, or friends—that something might be off, I know it's time to pivot. This is where my "ESPN" comes into play: Emotional, Situational, Personal, and Need.

The ESPN framework helps me pick up on emotional cues, identify the situation, and understand the personal needs that might be communicated—whether directly or indirectly.

One way I show love is through acts of service. It's just how I'm wired. By doing things for others, I express my love and care in a tangible way.

### Acts of Service: A Love Language in Action

One of the ways I express love and support in my marriage is through acts of service. Whether it's ironing something my wife needs, cooking dinner, cleaning the kitchen, washing dishes, or running errands, these actions are my way of showing her that I care. This servant-hearted approach isn't something I turn on and off—it's a natural part of who I am and how I contribute to my home. I believe that these small yet meaningful gestures help create a nurturing and supportive environment, reinforcing our bond and ensuring she feels valued and appreciated every day.

This same attitude extends to caring for my mom, who's now in her 80s. Whether it's moving things around for her or being there at a moment's notice when she calls, I do my best to show up for her. While I can't always be present every single time, the reality is that I'm deeply committed to serving those I love, especially when they need it most. Each act, whether big or small, reflects my dedication to supporting and caring for my family, emphasizing that love is not just a feeling but a series of deliberate actions.

### Supporting Others: A Parent's Duty

Beyond my immediate family, I also believe in extending support to those in need. Whether it's giving away a vehicle to a child in need, buying a car for someone, or offering financial assistance, these acts go beyond mere duty. They embody the essence of what it means to be a caring parent or loved one. To me, this is not just an obligation but a fundamental part of living out the values of empathy and generosity. It reflects the true spirit of parental and familial responsibility.

Servant leadership is more than just a concept; it's a way of life, particularly when deeply rooted in the TMC (Teach, Model, Coach) methodology. When you truly embrace TMC, it becomes part of your DNA—shaping how you engage with others, both in the workplace and at home. For me, this approach has seamlessly integrated into my daily life, influencing how I care for and support my family. It's about embodying the principles of servant leadership, ensuring that every action is guided by the desire to uplift and serve those around me.

## Balancing Leadership and Love at Home

There are times when my wife will remind me not to "coach" her, especially since she's heard me in action with clients and my leadership team. She's been right there, a passenger in my journey of growth, listening to countless conversations. So, when she says, "Don't TMC me right now," it's a light-hearted moment, but it's also a sign that she recognizes the influence of these practices in our relationship.

What's even more rewarding is when I see the positive impact of this servant leadership. The other night, while we were sitting on the couch, my wife turned to me out of the blue and said, "I love you. I really do love you." Those simple words were a powerful confirmation that the effort I put into our relationship—grounded in servant leadership—is not only recognized but deeply appreciated.

Servant leadership isn't just for home life—it extends to every interaction, including those with friends who are leaders in their own right. When I engage with them, I intentionally apply the TMC (Teach, Model, Coach) methodology in my communication. A key principle I follow is avoiding telling people what to do, especially when it comes to giving advice.

## Respecting Boundaries: The Art of Offering Advice

In my experience, men generally don't appreciate unsolicited advice—I know I don't, and I've seen many others share this sentiment. To address this, I've developed a respectful approach to my communication. Rather than pushing advice, I ask, "May I offer something to you?" When they agree, I don't provide direct instructions. Instead, I suggest they consider their situation from a different perspective, as if putting on a new set of lenses. This method allows them to explore alternative solutions without feeling pressured.

By encouraging others to view their challenges from a fresh angle, I'm not imposing my views but empowering them to make their own decisions. This approach respects their autonomy and acknowledges their leadership while fostering a collaborative spirit in our conversations. It's about creating an environment where they feel supported rather than directed, ensuring that our interactions are both constructive and respectful. This technique not only enhances our dialogue but also strengthens our relationships by valuing their perspectives and choices.

## The Power of Suggestion in Leadership

When I engage with others, especially fellow leaders, I've found that offering suggestions rather than directives makes a significant impact. Instead of telling someone what to do, I might say, "You may want to consider this," and then provide details on what I'm offering. This approach tends to be well-received because it respects the other person's autonomy and decision-making process.

By suggesting a different way to frame a situation, I'm not imposing my perspective but rather inviting them to explore alternatives. This method allows individuals to retain control over their lives and decisions, empowering them to create their own action plans or pivot as they see fit. It's about walking alongside them, offering insights, and then stepping back to let them decide what's best for them.

## The Ongoing Impact of TMC Methodology

This approach stems directly from the TMC (Teach, Model, Coach) methodology, which has profoundly shaped my communication style. TMC has taught me to guide without dictating and to suggest rather than command. This shift in approach hasn't just impacted my professional life; it has significantly transformed my personal interactions as well. By applying these principles, I've learned to support and empower others effectively, both at work and in my personal relationships.

The ability to offer advice respectfully and encourage others to view situations from different perspectives has fostered deeper, more collaborative relationships. It has enhanced my growth as a leader and a friend, extending the benefits of TMC far beyond the corporate environment. This methodology has become a cornerstone in how I engage with others, enriching my ability to connect, support, and lead in all areas of life.

## But Why It Matters

True leadership is about empowering others rather than controlling them. It's about fostering an environment where people feel supported and encouraged to make informed decisions. By offering suggestions and inviting others to consider different perspectives, we respect their autonomy and nurture their growth. This approach not only builds trust but also strengthens relationships by making individuals feel valued and understood.

Rooted in the TMC (Teach, Model, Coach) methodology, this form of leadership transcends traditional boundaries. It creates a culture of collaboration and mutual respect, where people are motivated to take ownership of their paths and contribute positively to their environments. This method helps in developing deeper, more meaningful connections and promotes a sense of shared purpose and achievement.

**Chapter 9 Key Points to Focus On:**

**Applying TMC (Teach, Model, Coach) at Home:**

The TMC methodology isn't just for the workplace. It's highly effective in personal relationships, particularly in marriage and family life, where listening, understanding, and supportive communication are key.

**Servant Leadership in Personal Relationships:**

Servant leadership extends to the home by valuing and serving others with love and empathy. Acts of service, rooted in genuine care, deepen relationships and create nurturing environments.

**Effective Communication through Suggestion and Empowerment:**

Respectful communication, especially in giving advice, fosters collaboration. By offering suggestions and encouraging new perspectives, relationships are strengthened, and autonomy is respected.

**Three-Step Action Plan:**

**Apply TMC in Your Personal Life:**

Action: Use the TMC approach in your marriage and family interactions. Focus on understanding communication styles, listening with empathy, and offering support.

Implementation: Be intentional in listening for emotional cues in conversations. Practice deeper engagement by asking questions that dig beneath the surface and reveal underlying feelings or concerns.

**Serve with Love and Acts of Service:**

Action: Incorporate acts of service into your daily life as expressions of love and care.

Implementation: Identify simple ways to serve your spouse, family, or friends regularly. Whether it's cooking, cleaning, or small acts of kindness, these actions may foster a nurturing atmosphere and strengthen bonds.

**Empower through Respectful Suggestions:**

Action: When offering advice, use suggestion-based communication to empower others to make their own decisions.

Implementation: The next time someone seeks your input, instead of directing them, offer a suggestion with phrases like, "You might want to consider..." This encourages them to think critically and take ownership of their actions.

By applying TMC principles in your personal life, serving with love, and empowering through respectful communication, you can enhance your relationships and create a supportive, growth-oriented home environment.

# Chapter 10:
# Sustaining The Transformation

Maintaining an optimistic and positive mindset is something people often ask me about. They want to know how I stay so upbeat and positive. The truth is, most of the time—around 90%—I genuinely do feel optimistic. But like everyone else, I have my moments of struggle, about 10% of the time, when challenges get the better of me.

The journey to developing this mindset wasn't easy, and it didn't happen overnight. It all started during a difficult time in my life—when I was dealing with the loss of my father. I noticed that the people around me, although well-intentioned, were speaking to me in a way that felt robotic and distant. They weren't trying to be hurtful; they were simply following the social script that our culture has ingrained in us. We are often conditioned to respond in certain ways during difficult times, but these responses can feel empty and unhelpful.

It was during this period that I had a powerful realization: If we have been programmed by our culture to think and respond in a certain way, then we have the power to reprogram ourselves. I decided to take control of how I communicate, how I perceive things, and how I respond to life's challenges. I didn't want to be a victim of my circumstances but rather an active participant in shaping my thoughts and emotions. This realization led me to develop what I now call the TMC (Transformational Mindset Conditioning) methodology. It's about reprogramming our minds to see the world differently, to respond with intention, and to communicate more meaningfully.

For me, this journey of reprogramming and growth is deeply rooted in my spiritual beliefs. There is no greater teacher than Jesus Christ. His teachings have guided me in this process of transformation, showing me how to approach life with love, patience, and faith. Through His example, I've learned that true optimism comes not from ignoring challenges but from facing them with the belief that we can overcome them and grow stronger in the process.

Navigating life is all about changing the lenses through which we view our experiences. For me, this shift began with how I dealt with my father's death. Losing him was one of the most traumatic events of my life—completely unexpected and devastating. But amidst the pain, I found an eye-opening realization: this was also an opportunity for growth. Instead of allowing the grief to consume me, I sought a deeper understanding of life, purpose, and resilience.

In searching for strength and guidance, I turned to my source—Jesus Christ. He is the foundation upon which I build my life, and His teachings are what sustain the methodology I live by Teach, Model, Coach (TMC). This approach is deeply rooted in His principles, which have guided me through every challenge, including my father's passing. The TMC methodology wasn't just an idea; it was born out of His example and the transformative power of faith.

When it comes to practical strategies for maintaining this mindset, I've developed a daily routine that keeps me grounded. Every morning, I wake up at three a.m. This early start is intentional, as it allows me to dedicate the first part of my day to connecting with God. I believe that starting the day in His presence sets the tone for everything that follows.

Every morning, my day begins at 3 a.m. sharp. This early start isn't just about getting a jump on the day; it's intentional time set aside to align my heart, mind, and spirit with God. Before I even rise from bed, I begin with an expression of gratitude. My first words are, "Thank you, Heavenly Father. Thank you, Jesus. Thank you, Holy Spirit." This act of thanksgiving sets the foundation for everything that follows.

Once I've acknowledged God's presence in my life, I get out of bed and head to the bathroom. I leave my phone there overnight, so it's the first thing I reach for once I'm up. Ready and waiting is the YouVersion Bible app's verse of the day—a small but impactful piece of scripture that sets a spiritual tone for my day.

Before diving in, I take a moment to nourish my body. I walk downstairs and pour myself a glass of ice-cold water. It's a simple act, but one that wakes me up physically, just as the Word of God awakens me spiritually. As I sip the water, I grab my headphones, ensuring that I'm fully focused and free from distractions when I begin my devotional time.

With the verse of the day playing through the app, I step outside for a few moments of peace. Letting my dogs out, I take in the stillness of the early morning as I reflect on the scripture. As they enjoy the fresh air, I'm savoring every word of the devotion, allowing it to speak into my life and guide my thoughts. By the time my dogs are ready to come back inside, I'm spiritually centered and ready for the next part of my morning ritual.

Next, I make myself a cup of tea—lemon ginger is my go-to. It's warming and soothing, another small ritual that grounds me. While the tea steeps, I move into the living room and settle into my favorite spot on the couch, where I spend the next portion of my morning nourishing my mind and spirit further.

I open YouTube, and the algorithm usually delivers just what I need—a sermon or motivational message from one of my trusted spiritual mentors: Dr. Tony Evans, Pastors Steven Furtick, Robert Morris, Craig Groeschel, or Michael Todd. These voices have a way of speaking directly to where I am in my journey. As the video plays, I allow the message to penetrate my thoughts, guiding and inspiring me as I prepare for the day ahead.

This routine is more than a habit; it's a lifeline. These messages reinforce my faith, providing wisdom and encouragement that aligns with my values. Occasionally, I feel led to share a message with someone I know who might need it. It's not a random act; it's intentional. If I feel a prompting from the Holy Spirit, I follow through, knowing that the right word at the right time can change someone's day, or even their life.

After the video, I often transition into a time of worship. I might play a worship song, allowing the lyrics to stir within me as I connect more deeply with God. Other times, I turn to the guided prayer feature on the YouVersion Bible app. This helps me focus my prayers, ensuring I'm covering different aspects of my life and my walk with God—whether it's seeking strength, guidance, or simply giving thanks.

Once this time of devotion is complete, I switch gears and prepare for the next part of my day—my workout. I get dressed and head out the door by 4:25 a.m. to meet with a group of like-minded men. Together, we start our session at 4:45 am with a devotion, setting the spiritual tone before we tackle our physical workout.

After the devotion we share our thoughts on the message, talk about how it applies to our lives, and lift one another up through encouragement with praise reports, and then prayer requests. We close that portion of our time together by praying as a group—a powerful act of unity that strengthens our bond and our faith. Then we workout. It's a routine that's not only about physical health but also about mental and spiritual resilience.

On Saturdays, my routine shifts a bit, but it still centers around the same core principles. I start by reading the verse of the day and listening to the YouVersion devotion, just like during the week. Then, I head to the gym—sometimes alone, sometimes with my wife—to get in a workout. It's a time for me to reflect, stay disciplined, and maintain that balance between mind, body, and spirit.

Sundays are a bit different. Instead of heading to the gym first thing, I go to church. Worshiping with my church family is an essential part of my spiritual life, and it's a time for renewal and growth. After church, I still make time to work out, keeping the physical routine consistent, but the focus of the day is on worship, resting, and honoring God.

Through these practices, I maintain a strong connection to Christ and continuously deepen my understanding of His teachings. By regularly immersing myself in scripture, worship, prayer, and reflection, I keep learning about His body of work—about empathy, grace, forgiveness, mercy, and gratitude. This holistic approach—spiritual, mental, and physical—keeps me aligned with His purpose for my life and equips me to face each day with faith, strength, and a heart full of gratitude.

I find myself constantly asking, "What would Christ do?" It's a simple yet profound question that keeps me grounded and focused on living a life that reflects His teachings. By continuously humbling myself in God's presence and striving to grow spiritually, I am reminded that this journey is not just about me. It's about following Christ's example, centering my life around His actions, and interacting with the world in a way that spreads light in places that may seem dark.

In a world that can often feel overwhelming and challenging, I feel a deep and passionate calling to stand in the gap and develop leaders who are committed to serving others. This is the essence of the Teach, Model, and Coach (TMC) methodology—a framework rooted in what Christ did and how He lived. It's about more than just leadership; it's about nurturing servant leaders who embody Christ's love, compassion, and humility.

When I reflect on the impact I've had on others through my YouTube channel, I can't help but think about the ripple effect that could be created if those individuals were also equipped with the TMC methodology. Imagine the potential if they, too, were empowered to teach, model, and coach others in their own communities. This multiplication effect could spread across households, zip codes, states, cultures, and families, creating a powerful movement of servant leadership.

This is why I'm so committed to this work. The TMC methodology isn't just a tool; it's a way of life that can transform not only individuals but entire communities.

Imagine, just for a moment, if we all took a step up in our ability to be true servant leaders. Picture how much better this world could be—starting with our neighborhoods, extending to our states, our country, and eventually, the entire world. It's a vision of unity, compassion, and purpose that could reshape everything we know. I can't help but reflect on this idea often, just as John Lennon once encouraged us to imagine a better world.

I recall hearing Dr. Tony Evans speak about how just a small group of people—nineteen, to be exact—completely changed the way the world travels. Those nineteen individuals, driven by a dark purpose, carried out the attacks of 9/11, and the impact of their actions was felt globally. It's staggering to think how such a small number of committed individuals could create such a profound shift in our world, altering how we live, how we move, and how we perceive safety.

Now, consider this: there are countless people who believe in Christ and understand His teachings of love, service, and unity. Yet, despite this shared belief, we often struggle to come together, to organize, and to bring about the kind of transformative change that could heal our world. We have the potential to create a movement grounded in the principles of servant leadership, but for some reason, we fall short of gathering that collective strength to make it happen.

It's mind-blowing to think about, isn't it? How can so few, united in a negative cause, bring about such a significant impact while so many of us, with a message of hope and love, struggle to make the same level of change? This realization is both challenging and inspiring.

I believe my true calling is to stand in the gaps where leadership falls short, especially within large corporations and organizations. So many people go home after work carrying the weight of their day—baggage that is often heavy and negative. Unfortunately, this burden doesn't stay at the office. It follows them home, spilling over into their personal lives affecting how they interact with their loved ones. They may become short-tempered, withdrawn, or simply too exhausted to be fully present. When people feel overworked, devalued, and unappreciated, it takes a toll on their well-being, and that ripple effect can harm families and communities.

Now, imagine if we could change that. Imagine if people came home from work filled with joy because they felt seen, heard, and valued in their workplace. Picture the difference it would make if their work environment was a source of encouragement and growth rather than stress and frustration. When people are treated with respect and appreciation, they bring that positivity home. They're more patient, more loving, and more engaged with their families. This shift could create a domino effect, spreading hope and resilience throughout entire communities.

Imagine the potential we have to spread HOPE - *helping other people endure,* overcoming their challenges with greater strength. Picture the HOPE – *helping other people excel*, and how we could empower people to excel in every aspect of their lives, not just at work but also in their homes and relationships. This vision of servant leadership isn't just about improving the workplace; it's about transforming lives. It's about creating a culture where people thrive both professionally and personally. When leaders are intentional about valuing and uplifting their teams, the impact extends far beyond the office walls. It reaches into homes, strengthens families, and builds communities rooted in hope, joy, and mutual respect.

This is why I believe I'm here—to provide HOPE – *help open people's eyes*, through servant leadership and guiding them to their true potential. The Teach, Model, and Coach methodology isn't just about professional development; it's also about fostering personal growth. By integrating these principles, you can transform not only your work life but also your personal life, creating a more fulfilling and balanced existence.

If you're interested in exploring this further or would like me to facilitate workshops for your team or provide one-on-one coaching, please don't hesitate to reach out. You can visit my website at **troycsmith-hope.com** to connect with me or find me on various social media platforms. I'm here to support you in your journey toward growth and leadership.

Remember, hope is a powerful force. It stands for "Hold On, Pain Ends." Whether you're feeling stuck or seeking to enhance your leadership skills, my goal is to offer guidance and encouragement to those who are hurting. May God bless you and your loved ones, and may you experience continuous and intentional growth in your journey toward becoming a servant leader.

**Chapter 10 Key Points to Focus On:**

**Optimism and Mindset Reprogramming:**

The development of a positive and optimistic mindset involves intentional reprogramming, drawing on faith and resilience. It's about choosing to respond intentionally to life's challenges rather than being a victim of circumstances.

**Daily Rituals for Spiritual, Mental, and Physical Alignment:**

Daily practices rooted in faith, such as starting the day with prayer, scripture, and reflection, are essential for maintaining a strong connection with God and staying centered in His teachings.

**The Ripple Effect of Servant Leadership:**

Servant leadership, particularly through the Teach, Model, and Coach (TMC) methodology, has the potential to create a ripple effect, transforming not only the workplace but also personal lives and communities.

**Three-Step Action Plan:**

**Reprogram Your Mindset with Faith:**

Action: Embrace challenges as opportunities for growth and reprogram your mind to focus on optimism and resilience.

Implementation: Whenever a difficult situation arises, pause and reflect on how you can approach it with faith and positivity. Reframe your perspective by asking, "How can this experience help me grow?"

**Establish a Morning Ritual for Alignment:**

Action: Develop a consistent morning routine that nurtures your spiritual, mental, and physical well-being.

Implementation: Begin each day with gratitude and prayer. Set aside time for scripture reading, reflection, and physical exercise to align your heart, mind, and body before the demands of the day begin.

**Spread the Ripple Effect of Servant Leadership:**

Action: Apply the TMC methodology to create a ripple effect of servant leadership in your community and workplace.

Implementation: Focus on teaching, modeling, and coaching others by leading with empathy, compassion, and humility. Intentionally invest in developing others' growth and well-being, inspiring them to do the same for those around them.

By reprogramming your mindset, cultivating a morning ritual, and practicing servant leadership, you can sustain personal transformation while positively impacting others.

www.ingramcontent.com/pod-product-compliance
Lightning Source LLC
Chambersburg PA
CBHW020123180726
47992CB00020B/2184